PRAISE FOR
THE CULTURAL PROFICIENCY MANIFESTO

"'The failure to have curriculum and instruction that portrays our history in authentic ways and represents our society inclusively illustrates a form of educational malpractice that ill equips educators and our students to function effectively in our country.' This is just one topic in this manifesto that empowers the courageous leader to stop perpetuating the status quo and engage in creating a culturally proficient school system. It is a call to action for educators to ensure that we are creating culturally responsive educational environments as a reaction to the 'noise' emanating from the 2016 election cycle and its aftermath. Culturally proficient educators create classrooms and schoolwide conditions to support all learners achieving at levels higher than ever before.' It provides focus and clarity about what really matters in schools—our students. Regardless of who knocks on our schoolhouse doors, it is our moral imperative to educate all students, and this book teaches us how to authentically engage in the work of educating our wonderfully diverse population."

Dr. Julie A. Vitale, Superintendent
Romoland School District

"Dr. Lindsey makes a clear and passionate case for the need for social justice to be moved to the forefront for all of us. He makes it an imperative to move beyond words to actions and to become leaders in providing an equitable future for all."

Raymond Terrell, Interim Chair Teacher (Education)
Miami University of Ohio

"This latest book by Randall B. Lindsey offers educators paths to hope in the 'new normal' following the 2016 elections. Amidst the cacophony of this 'noise' he challenges us to surface privilege and entitlements through tools of cultural proficiency in the service of all students. All educators owe it to themselves and the children they teach to rise above the 'noise' and find the clarity this book offers."

Dr. Rosemary Papa, Professor of Comparative and
International Education and Leadership
Soka University of America

"Professional development and dialogue around the tools of The Cultural Proficiency Manifesto *provide a bridge to support school leaders in developing a relationship with their community as they improve access and equity to quality education for America's children."*

Dr. Patricia Horton, Principal
Colton Joint Unified School District

"A must-read for those perplexed with the current political rhetoric. Through an autobiographical approach, Dr. Lindsey brings clarity of purpose and productive action in creating an environment where ALL students can be successful."

Dr. Luis A. Rankins-Ibarra, Superintendent of Schools
Escondido Union School District

"Powerful, genuine, personal, and supportive, the author rallies all educators to view cultural differences as assets, have hope, and dedicate themselves to moving forward using culturally proficient practices."

Dr. Jaime E. Welborn, Assistant Professor
(Education Leadership)

"Powerfully moving! Randall B. Lindsey provides a stirring appeal to stand on the platform of cultural proficiency to quiet the 'noise' and make the necessary changes to fully educate each child. We are already able, we simply need to do!"

Franklin Campbell Jones, Vice President
Campbell Jones and Associates

"The timing of Dr. Lindsey's book could not be more perfect or more necessary. It allows us to slow down, re-engage, and reflect on where we have been, where we are now, and where we want to go. It pushes against our comfort zone in a way that invites us to explore and challenge our beliefs, while 'becoming aware and knowing what you don't know.' Finally, it reminds us that this is a journey of introspection and continuous growth for educators committed to educating ALL children."

Dr. Nancy Dome, CEO
Epoch Education

"Now more important than ever, Randall B. Lindsey provides us the why, what, and how to continually strive to be individually and collectively culturally proficient! Why? As educators, we must meet our moral imperative to create a socially just democracy by educating all of our children in all of our schools! What? Creating a socially just democracy requires educators and schools who constantly develop their individual and collective knowledge, understanding, and skills of cultural proficiency. How? Skillful and honest use of the Culturally Proficient Framework, Guiding Principles, Continuum Rubric, Essential Elements, and Cultural Proficiency Tools will systematically facilitate culturally proficient students, educators, and schools."

Dr. Bess Scott, Associate Professor of Educational Leadership
Doane University

"Dr. Lindsey's latest book is a critical must-read for socially conscious educational leaders and citizens who care deeply about the future viability and vitality of their communities as well as the sustainability of our deep democratic

ideals. The Manifesto encourages concerned people from all backgrounds to nurture their own passions for justice and equal opportunity for all, and provides valuable strategies for personal and systemic reflection and collective action that is as imperative now as any time in our nation's history. The Manifesto offers practical tools for generating productive dialogues that help all of us move from silence and inaction to discussion and action on sticky challenges of difference and diversity. Most urban, suburban, and rural communities throughout my region are experiencing relatively rapid, and in some cases unexpected, racial, ethnic, economic, and political demographic changes. Many school leaders and educators and the 'new' diverse communities they serve are actively seeking support and guidance on how to better support students that have traditionally struggled in our schools, and the Manifesto offers important tools for building inclusive educational environments that are truly responsive to the learning, social-emotional, and cultural needs of their increasingly diverse student bodies. Dr. Lindsey and his colleagues have amassed a significant body of work on Culturally Proficient living and learning over the past 20 years that has provided the framework for transformational practice for thousands of educators, law enforcement officials, and community activists throughout the country. Dr. Lindsey's most recent effort offers those of us who regularly support school and district leaders an important guide to creating systemic reflection and change, thereby breaking down visible and invisible barriers to educational equity. The Manifesto is an impactful study guide for educators in their own cultural proficiency journey, and more importantly a guide for creating meaningful change in both policy and practice that ultimately opens doors of opportunity and possibility to those students who have traditionally been designated to the margins of success in our schools and society."

Dr. Robert L. Jarvis, Director of Equity Leadership Initiatives
Penn Center for Educational Leadership
University of Pennsylvania

"This 'manifesto' is indeed timely and essential. Dr. Lindsey's vast experience as an expert and leader in the field of cultural proficiency reminds us that 'now is the time' to acknowledge and address the vast number of diversity, equity, and social justice issues at hand. His hope is my hope . . . his clarity is all our clarity."

Dr. Kenneth R. Magdaleno, Executive Director
Center for Leadership, Equity, and Research (CLEAR)

The Cultural Proficiency Manifesto

To Delores B. Lindsey—
Together on our journey toward Cultural Proficiency

The Cultural Proficiency Manifesto

Finding Clarity Amidst the Noise

Manifesto: A statement of policy that might inform our actions as educators

Randall B. Lindsey

Foreword by Stephanie Graham Rivas

CORWIN
A SAGE Publishing Company

FOR INFORMATION:

Corwin

A SAGE Company

2455 Teller Road

Thousand Oaks, California 91320

(800) 233-9936

www.corwin.com

SAGE Publications Ltd.

1 Oliver's Yard

55 City Road

London EC1Y 1SP

United Kingdom

SAGE Publications India Pvt. Ltd.

B 1/I 1 Mohan Cooperative Industrial Area

Mathura Road, New Delhi 110 044

India

SAGE Publications Asia-Pacific Pte. Ltd.

3 Church Street

#10-04 Samsung Hub

Singapore 049483

Acquisitions Editor: Dan Alpert

Associate Editor: Lucas Schleicher

Production Editor: Bennie Clark Allen

Copy Editor: Alison Hope

Typesetter: C&M Digitals (P) Ltd.

Proofreader: Eleni-Maria Georgiou

Indexer: Jeanne Busemeyer

Cover Designer: Scott Van Atta

Marketing Manager: Charline Maher

Printed in the United States of America

ISBN: 978-1-5063-9937-9

This book is printed on acid-free paper.

SUSTAINABLE FORESTRY INITIATIVE

Certified Chain of Custody
Promoting Sustainable Forestry
www.sfiprogram.org
SFI-01268

SFI label applies to text stock

17 18 19 20 21 10 9 8 7 6 5 4 3 2 1

Contents

Foreword   xiii
 Stephanie Graham Rivas

Acknowledgments   xv

About the Author   xvii

Introduction   1

PART I: THE NOISE: A VICIOUS CYCLE   5

Chapter 1: Purpose of This Manifesto   7
 My Perspective   8
 My Concern   10
 Reflection   11
 The Cultural Proficiency Framework as a Road Map   11
 Technical and Adaptive Change   14
 Reflection   15
 Expressions of Bigotry *Can* Be Motivational   16
 Reflection   17
 Design of This Book   18

Chapter 2: A Brief History of Inequity and
Equity: A Tsunami Warning   19
 Lesson Learned #1   20
 Cycles of Disruption as Levers for Change: A Tsunami Warning   21
 Inequities Are on Our Doorsteps for Us to Address   22
 The Silver Lining of Equity in Our Founding Documents   24
 Lesson Learned #2   25
 Reflection   25
 Reflection   26
 More About Achievement Gaps   26
 The Myth of Failing Public Schools   27
 School Reform from 1980s to Present   29
 Going Deeper   30
 Dialogic Activity   30

Chapter 3: History and Hope for Changing Schools   **33**

Education Language and the Power of "Why?"   33
Lesson Learned #3   34
Transformative Change   36
The Achievement Gap Is Not New   36
Into the Second Century of Education Reform:
   The "Why?" Question   37
Amidst the Noise Is Clarity   38
Going Deeper   39
Dialogic Activity   39

PART II: LISTENING FOR CLARITY   **41**

Chapter 4: The Cultural Proficiency Framework   **43**

Culturally Proficient Leadership   43
Lesson Learned #4   45
The Tools of Cultural Proficiency   46
The Cultural Proficiency Conceptual Framework as a Guide   47
Barriers vs. Cultural Assets: The Tension for Change   47
Transforming the Culture of School   50
Going Deeper   51
Dialogic Activity   51

**Chapter 5: Resistance to Change: The
Anger–Guilt Continuum**   **53**

Surfacing Privilege and Entitlement   54
Reflections on Entitlement: A Mystic Elementary
   School Conversation   57
Reflective Activity   59
Carrying Our Learning Forward   59
Going Deeper   63
Dialogic Activity   63

**Chapter 6: Going Forward Takes Commitment
and Effort: It Always Has**   **65**

The Blaring of Trumpets   67
PHASE 1: The Guiding Principles of Cultural Proficiency   68
Nine Key Questions for Reflection and Dialogue   68
Use Internal Assets and Be Intentional   72
PHASE 2: The Essential Elements of Cultural Competence   72
Going Deeper   77
Dialogic Activity   78

Chapter 7: My Final Thoughts and, Then, Your Turn   **79**
    Two-Phase Process—Guiding Principles and Essential Elements   80
    Reflection   81
    Closing Comments   82

References   **83**

Resources   **85**

Index   **97**

Foreword

'Amid the Noise is Clarity.'
Randall B. Lindsey's Call To Action

The previously published books about Cultural Proficiency (Corwin Press) have been gifts to educators and other professionals wanting to know the "what's" and "how's" of personal and organizational cultural proficiency. These books have served their users well with a framework and tools to help them begin the work, stay on course and monitor their progress. In **The Cultural Proficiency Manifesto: Finding Clarity Amidst the Noise,** Lindsey has made the most compelling argument yet for taking the self and others on a quest for cultural proficiency by anchoring the quest in the "why" of the work. *Why* do we do it? *Why* must we do it? And *why* do and should we persist? The first two chapters ground readers in the history of equity and inequity in this nation, the trials, tribulations, progress and set-backs, and the unfinished work which has paved the way for our on-going struggle for equity and justice and evolving our democracy to be what our founding fathers intended. *Why* do we do this work? Because we are nowhere near finished with the work started in the early years of this nation's quest for civil rights and justice. *Why* must we do it? Because diversity is this nation's greatest strength, but our outcomes are perniciously disparate for some demographic groups. *Why* should we persist? Because recent political uncertainty and upheaval in our country and for many of our global allies threaten to erode, if not reverse, much of the progress made by too many brave activists and advocates before us. These are the *whys* for this work, and they do not allow us to give up, stop, or retire from the work. For Lindsey, knowing the *whys* for this work makes us persist even when we encounter setbacks, roadblocks and reversals.

For the many who emerged from the 2016 election disillusioned, embittered or paralyzed by the aftermath of confusion, distractions and chaos, Lindsey's advice is to harness the current cycles of disruption as levers for change, to embolden our stance and empower our speech, and by so doing, we can find hope and renewed inspiration for moving forward as a profession and as a country.

Stephanie Graham Rivas

Acknowledgments

Two or three places in this book you will notice that I make reference to my Corwin colleague, friend, and editor, Dan Alpert. Consistent with the Corwin ethos, Dan represents a personal and professional commitment to social justice. Dan and I have a practice of talking five or six times a year, mostly to check in about family and to talk about trends in PreK–12 education. As you will read in this book, it was one of those chats that led to Dan suggesting the idea for this book.

Parts of this book are derived from earlier works, principally what I refer to in shorthand as the "Schools" and the "Common Core" books. My appreciation goes to Franklin Campbell Jones and the late Laraine Roberts, for without them the book would never have been conceptualized, in particular the sections on Privilege and Entitlement. Appreciation also to Delores Lindsey, Karen Kearney, and Delia Estrada for allowing me to "pull forward" the leadership material from the "Common Core" book and, in particular, for being able to adapt and repurpose the Rubric for Culturally Proficient Learning.

Once the draft manuscript was complete, I invited several experts in the field of socially just education to provide critical friend feedback. Provide critical friend feedback they did! I am grateful for their attention to concept and detail. Without the encouragement and engagement of these many colleagues and friends, this book would still be just a concept in my head and a passion in my heart. As with earlier manuscripts, I relied on coauthors to read and to provide corrections and suggestions. Once again, Delores Lindsey, Raymond Terrell, and Diana Stephens provided indispensable feedback, both big picture and attention to details. Carita Green, administrator with Minnesota School District 196, and Peter Flores III, administrator with Santa Maria (California) Joint Union High School District provided on-the-ground feedback intended to ensure the book's utility in the local school context. A special thank you to attorneys Erin Bradrick and Aditya Ajwani. I have known Erin all her life and truly appreciate her and Aditya's (as well as Dan's) prompting me to insert more of my "voice" into the manuscript.

About the Author

Randall B. Lindsey, PhD, is emeritus professor, California State University, Los Angeles, and has a practice centered on educational consulting and issues related to equity and access. Prior to higher education faculty roles, Randy served as a junior and senior high school history teacher, a district office administrator for school desegregation, and executive director of a nonprofit corporation. All of Randy's experiences have been in working with diverse populations, and his area of study is the behavior of white people in multicultural settings. It is his belief and experience that too often members of dominant groups are observers of cross-cultural issues rather than personally involved with them. He works with colleagues to design and implement programs for and with schools and community-based organizations to provide access and achievement.

With coauthors Kikanza Nuri Robins and Raymond Terrell, Randall published the initial Cultural Proficiency book, *Cultural Proficiency: A Manual for School Leaders,* now in its 3rd edition (2009) for Corwin. His most recent books, also with Corwin, include *Culturally Proficient Collaboration: The Use and Misuse of School Counselors* (with Diana L. Stephens, 2011); an edited volume titled *The Best of Corwin: Equity* (2012); *Culturally Proficient Practice: Supporting Educators of English Learning Students* (with Reyes Quezada and Delores Lindsey, 2012); and *A Culturally Proficient Response to the Common Core: Ensuring Equity Through Professional Learning* (with Delores B. Lindsey, Karen M. Kearney, Delia Estrada, and Raymond D. Terrell, 2015). Randall published a chapter titled "Culturally

Proficient Leadership: Doing What's Right for Students—All Students" (with coauthor Raymond Terrell, 2015) in *Key Questions for Educational Leaders,* edited by John P. Portelli and Darrin Griffiths and published by Words and Deeds. Randy and his wife and frequent coauthor, Delores, are enjoying this phase of life as grandparents, as educators, and in support of a just cause.

Introduction

I know a thing or two because I have seen a thing or two!

—Line from a TV ad for Farmer's Insurance

In August 2016 I had the opportunity to spend the day with middle school educators and introduce them to the Tools of Cultural Proficiency. It was my further pleasure to be copresenting with two colleagues, Joseph Domingues and Peter Flores III, administrators in the neighboring Santa Maria Joint Union High School District. Our middle school participants were enthusiastic in embracing the concepts and strategies of Cultural Proficiency. Late in the afternoon a group of teachers were talking while they enjoyed the social break. They were concerned about the influence that the negative tone of the 2016 election cycle might have in their classrooms. Mostly, they didn't know how to cope. I listened and asked a few questions about their concerns. For a few minutes we talked about their school climate concerns. Joe, Pete and I reconvened the session and facilitated a dialogue about the importance of expressing inclusive core values that are lived by both the educators and the students. The teachers spoke about the need for seamless connections between the school's core values and the educators' actions. The teachers were quite clear about walking the talk.

On my five-hour drive home that evening, I listened to news reports describing instances of hate-filled graffiti on school walls and of students seemingly mimicking intemperate comments made by presidential candidates. In listening to the radio reports and reflecting on the concerns expressed by the middle school educators earlier in the day, I had a sense of déjà vu. Over the next few days I talked with Delores Lindsey and Raymond Terrell, who, like me, had led desegregation efforts with school districts in Illinois, Ohio, and Louisiana. I asked if they, upon hearing the news reports about schools, were also experiencing this sense of déjà vu when hearing news reports about students' and some educators' intemperate comments and actions. They answered with a decided *Yes!*

The restive undercurrents of today are strikingly similar to the pushback we experienced in the 1970s. We *had* been here before! Hence, my choice of epigraph to open this essay! Since that August professional development, Delores and I in our work with PreK–12 schools and our university course began to share with colleagues that the 2016 election cycle appeared to be surfacing tensions that were cyclical in nature. As a teacher of U.S. history, I am well aware that a subtext of our country's story is the too often ignored theme of exploitation and systemic oppression based on superiority–inferiority conceptions of racial, ethnic, socioeconomic, gender, faith, and sexual orientation differences.

As a social justice educator, I have served as a high school history teacher with two school districts, as a district-level administrator for desegregation in two school districts, and as an education professor at four universities. The social justice nature of my professional roles has led me to learn how little many of our educator colleagues, let alone parents in the schools we serve, realize that the social divisions of today are deeply rooted in past inequities. I often hear comments such as, "Why don't "they" just get over it? Let's move forward!"

Shortly after the election and inauguration (2016–17), our Corwin friend, colleague, and editor, Dan Alpert, and I were lamenting the uncivil discourse arising in our schools and across society when Dan suddenly suggested, "Randy, you should write a manifesto to guide educators through this morass!" Dan proceeded to describe the concomitant nature of the body of work that my coauthors and I had amassed, my roles as a teacher and administrator, and educators' need for a policy-based approach to access and equity. The idea was to describe the historical and cyclical nature of the expressions of bias and hate. It was my opinion that educators equipped with this historical knowledge would be intentional in developing policies and practices in our schools and values and behaviors among our educator colleagues that would interrupt the cycle of hostility directed toward historically marginalized groups. It took me very little time to agree to develop my ideas for the manifesto! Over the next few weeks, I reviewed our books, consulted other sources of information, and outlined the manifesto. From the Cultural Proficiency books, I have drawn on the Privilege and Entitlement material from *Culturally Proficient Schools*, second edition (2013) and *A Culturally Proficient Response to the Common Core* (2015).

The first day I sat at my desk to put pen to paper (actually, fingers to keys) was January 16, 2017. Late in the day when I took a break from working the keys, I noted the significance of the date. The connection of celebrating Dr. King's birthday and his work to the writing I had ahead of me was not lost in that moment.

In constructing this book I began listening to varied voices and their topics:

- Those who speak of a postracial society
- The rise of the Tea Party
- The rise of Black Lives Matter

- Voter suppression efforts
- Police brutality and allegations of police brutality
- Islamophobia
- Anti-Semitism
- Persistent attention to educational disparities
- Postassimilationist society
- Resurgent white nationalism

This book is not about those things. This book is about working together in ways that enables our country to becoming an inclusive democracy.

As you will see in Part I, our country is on a trajectory in which civil rights and responsibilities are ever expanding. We are where we are today because of the efforts of our predecessors. This book provides you a template to guide you and your school/district's intentional movement for inclusivity so that all students have access to high-level curriculum, instruction, and outcomes.

This book extends to you and your colleagues Cross's (1989) inside-out personal and institutional approach to deep transformative change. Education is one institution with the capacity for both educators and their schools to be transformative simultaneously. Inclusivity and equity are goals attained only through intentional actions.

Educators and schools have information today not available to previous generations. Since the desegregation efforts of the 1960s and 1970s the topics of inequity and achievement disparities have become known and slowly embraced throughout our profession.

The National Assessment of Educational Progress (NAEP) has been reporting about demographic group inequities in reading and mathematics achievement since the mid 1970s and has made those reports available to school districts nationwide. It was not until 2002 and what I refer to as the "silver lining" in No Child Left Behind (NCLB) that disaggregated student achievement data became prominent topics of discussion in school districts across the country. The proverbial cat was out of the bag. My purpose here it not to litigate the past and ask who knew what and when did they know it. Rather than be mired in the past, I encourage us to take our collective heads out of the sand and recognize that now we are supported by several encouraging elements for moving forward and creating inclusive schools where students succeed because of their cultural memberships, not in spite of them. We now know the following to be true:

- Students from all demographic groups can achieve at high levels.
- Educators have the capacity and the ability to educate students from all demographic groups.
- Templates for moving forward exist and might be best exemplified by Asa Hilliard's provocative question: "Do we have the will to educate all children?" (Hilliard, 1991, p. 36).
- The skill and knowledge exist to do the work of educating all children and youths. The will to do the work is ours to grasp.

Lessons Learned

On four occasions through the chapters that follow I insert a section titled "Lesson Learned." The intent of these brief statements is to share with you what I am learning on my Cultural Proficiency journey. Your lessons learned could be different. The important thing, I believe, is that to be effective in our increasingly diverse society, educational leaders must recognize their and their schools assets in educating our country's children and youths. Likewise, to be effective it is as important for our educational leaders to recognize their areas of needed improvement in preparing our children and youths to live in an inclusive, diverse country.

So, what are we waiting for? Let's get to work.

PART I

The Noise:
A Vicious Cycle

Forgiveness does not forget the past,
but it does enlarge the future.

—Paul Boese (1967, p. 146)

In Chapter 1 I discuss the purpose of this manifesto. I describe my perspective and my concern. I introduce the Cultural Proficiency Framework, a bit about technical and adaptive change, bigotry as a pivot point, and the design of this book. Chapter 2 provides a brief history of inequity and equity as a context for the "noise" emanating from the 2016 election cycle and its aftermath. The chapter also introduces two of my lessons learned that I offer not so much as examples for you to emulate but more to encourage you, as an educational leader, to be continuously engaged as a learner striving to meet the needs of our diverse school communities. Chapter 3 presents our history as reason for hope in moving forward as a profession and as a country. Chapter 3 closes with my belief that "Amidst the Noise Is Clarity."

CHAPTER 1

Purpose of
This Manifesto

I have hope for our country. More specifically, I have hope for the education profession. I begin with expressions of hope because of the noise that has surfaced in our country. Racist chatter, ethnic and religious-based name calling, graffiti on mosques and synagogues, desecration of Jewish cemeteries, bomb threats to Jewish community centers, and assaults on people who are gay, lesbian, bisexual, and transgender have reemerged. I recognize these incidents as a part of the historic fabric of our country too often unrecognized and, therefore, unacknowledged. For progress to be made, it begins with you and me recognizing there is a problem. It begins with us—you and me—recognizing hate and bigotry as our problem as leaders to address; it doesn't matter who we are.

The rancor and discord unleashed by the 2016 election cycle poses risks that, when viewed as part of a recurring historical cycle, can be posed as opportunities for our schools. Expressions of racial, ethnic, and gender-based bigotry and hate must be acknowledged as real, not transitory, and reframed in terms of next steps that educators and our schools and school districts might take in providing high-quality inclusive educational opportunities and outcomes for all of our students. The United States of America will not become less diverse. Diversity is our present and our future. Now is the time, and opportunity is at hand to mold the vision of our diverse country as a place where one's cultural characteristics are viewed and embraced as assets and not as deficits. One's race, ethnicity, gender, faith, social class, sexual orientation, sexual identity, and the various intersections make us who we are as individuals and as a country. Our profession as educators puts us in position to be leaders in our country's evolution in being inclusive. It has not been easy to this point so, please, don't think it gets any easier. I'll bet there was at least one important person in your life that echoed for you what my father intoned on numerous occasions: "Anything worth having in life takes effort."

Yes, developing facility with strategies designed to interrupt hate speech or to promote dialogue among discordant voices is very important. With this manifesto I appeal for you to listen beneath the noise and to recognize the range of voices that have been unleashed. Some voices are calling for the expulsion or imprisonment of others and are in stark contrast to voices of the aggrieved. The voices of the aggrieved must not be confused or conflated with the voices trying to shout them down. In responding to the noise, we must not be seduced into approaches that paper over differences in order to "just get along." Now is an opportune time in our nation's history to dig more deeply into our own personal values and into our schools' and school districts' core values to promote intergroup understanding and provide equitable educational opportunity and outcomes for all students in our schools.

All Who Dare to Proceed Will Benefit. For sake of illustration, I propose that we array educators along a diversity-type spectrum. At one end of the spectrum are people who view our society as politically correct in dealing with cultural differences, while at the other end are educators who regard society as irreparably oppressive. My experience is that most educators are not aligned with extreme views but are concerned by the tumult that arose from the 2016 election cycle. I write this book as a means for interested parties to seize this moment and to guide deep-thinking educators, irrespective of where they might be along this spectrum, to engage in reflection and dialogue activities. In doing so participants have the opportunity to develop mindsets for them and their schools being successful in educating children and youths from across the demographic spectrum. The opportunity is before us and is ours to seize.

Historic and systemic oppression is part of our country's history and repeats in cyclical fashion. We can embrace this cycle of rancor as an on-ramp to **opportunities for extending the benefits of education equitably to all demographic sectors of our vast and varied nation.**

MY PERSPECTIVE

More than five months have passed since our November 2016 general election. I'm taking this moment to look back on my own history as well as our nation's history to learn more about who I am in the context of our country's greater history and what you and I can do as educators to move forward with purpose and intention.

This is my fifty-second year as an educator. I am a member of the ascendant middle class. My parents were teenagers during the 1930s, in the era of the Great Depression. My father as a nineteen-year-old enlisted in the Civilian Conservation Corps where he served for three and a half years. In his words, he was taking a mouth away from the table. My mother worked part-time for governmental relief agencies. My parents were hard-working people. My father worked forty years in a factory and my mother was a stay-at-home mom until my sister and I graduated high school, after which she worked as a sales clerk. I am a first-generation high school and college graduate.

I was in a college sociology class when I learned our family was considered low income, information based on parental education and jobs. Taken aback by that evaluation and revelation, I asked my father about his take on my new learning. Though Dad stopped his education after the eighth grade because he knew the family couldn't afford clothing for high school, he remains one of the most learned people I have known. His smiling response was, "No, we are not poor. There just never is any extra money."

My first job earning a paycheck was as our school custodian's helper when I was fourteen years old. I worked before and after school and a half-day on Saturdays, and forty-hour weeks during the summers. I was very fortunate as a freshman and sophomore high school student to have a job. I continued with part-time jobs at grocery stores until I graduated high school. Having a wage-earning job allowed me to experience independence early in my life. Also, having a job allowed me to select and pay for my own clothing, which took pressure off the family budget. I was not a lot different from many of my 1950s small-town mid-America male and female classmates. Most of us held part-time jobs.

Dad reminded me I was among the first in his and mom's family to actually finish high school. I was very fortunate to begin my college experience in 1960 as President Eisenhower's signature infrastructure accomplishment, the Interstate Highway System, was being constructed across the country. Having the opportunity for well-paid construction jobs afforded me the opportunity to attend and graduate from university loan free. Little did I know at the time that these early life experiences would shape my worldview about the socioeconomics of educational equity.

I began my career as a teacher of social studies to ninth-grade junior high school students in Kankakee, Illinois. I have taught at two high schools (Illinois and California) and have served as an administrator of school desegregation in two school districts (Illinois and Ohio). The second decade of my career led me to university-level teaching where my primary focus has been school leadership for social justice. I am not a particularly religious person but if I were, I am most swayed by Buddhist and Jesuit commitments to social justice.

I share these snippets of the progression of my career so that, early on, you are very clear about the purpose and intent of this book: it is to make the case that we, as educators, possess the necessary information and skills to successfully educate children and youths from all demographic groups (i.e., racial, ethnic, gender, social class, gender identity/expression). More than twenty-five years ago the late Professor Asa Hilliard (1991) posed the provocative question that appears as an epigraph to Part I and continues to guide me to this day: "Do we have the will to educate all children?" I believe with all my energy that the vast majority of us in this profession possess the skills of curriculum, instruction, and assessment. The *will* to educate all children is developed when we embrace the moral aspects of our work—from the classroom, to the school level, to the district level. When we embrace the notion that all students can learn and we can teach them all, then we are capable of educating all students.

MY CONCERN

The rancor and hatred, let alone the viciousness, unleashed by dynamics surrounding the 2016 election primaries and general election and aftermath pain me. For me, a subtext to the campaigns began with the noise I heard from the general population via television and social media. Following that, I heard noise from schools and classrooms across the country. Finally, I began to hear noise in my own family.

The noise that I hear carries with it sometimes subtle, other times direct, expressions of racism, sexism, misogyny, heterosexism, anti-Semitism, Islamophobia, and xenophobia. All of these give rise to oppression that, when allowed to go unchecked in our nation's history, has led to loss of civil liberties and loss of life itself. It is as if a festering boil has been pricked again and suppressed forms of poison have erupted.

A call to action. I use the term "noise" as an indicator for "listen up." We must use this noise as our rallying call to action. My focus for this book is confined to my role of educator. This manifesto is my rallying call to other educators who are compelled to move forward using culturally proficient practices focused on socially just classrooms, schools, and school districts.

In these first two decades of the twenty-first century our profession has made progress in educating Pre-K to twelfth-grade students to ever-higher levels of academic progress. I hasten to add, though, that the progress is uneven. The progress is *very* uneven. Yet there is progress and it is our challenge to stay in the game. To achieve an inclusive democracy aligned with goals of democratic public schooling we cannot—no, we must not—let societal rancor and divisiveness impede our goal of providing inclusive schooling practices for all children and youths. Rather, the rancor should shake us into action.

My design with this manifesto is, first, to reflect on our country's progress in providing access to the benefits of our democracy in increasingly inclusive ways, with particular emphasis on educational opportunities. In doing so I illustrate progress made and barriers that exist and persist, and I focus on the future of what can be.

With the backdrop of historical challenges met and real progress that continues, the Cultural Proficiency Framework is presented in Chapter 4 as a road map for lessening the noise. Raymond Terrell, Kikanza Nuri Robins, and I adapted Terry Cross's (1989) Cultural Competence model for social work to the PreK–12 school context. We learned of his work while directing the Regional Assistance Center for Educational Equity, a U.S. Department of Education–funded desegregation center at California State University, Los Angeles. From Cross's approach we observed an open, unambiguous depiction of historical and current barriers to equity in schools that could be countered by core values and standards, when applied to schools, could lead to narrowing access and achievement gaps that persist in our schools and school districts.

REFLECTION

Have you noticed the levels of noise that I describe? What is your reaction? If you have not noticed the noise I describe, what is your reaction to my description? Please use the space below to enter your responses.

_____

_____

_____

THE CULTURAL PROFICIENCY FRAMEWORK AS A ROAD MAP

The Cultural Proficiency Framework arranges Cross's (1989) Tools of Cultural Proficiency into a scaffold to guide your movement forward as an educator and to help you lead an equity focus for your school or school district. The two major functions of the Framework are providing tools to support the clarification of your and your school's core values in educating students from diverse communities; and providing tools for guiding your behaviors and developing your school's policies and practices to be inclusive of students from diverse communities. School district leaders across the United States and Canada are using the Framework to guide their planning and consequent actions in addressing identified inequities in student access to high-level thinking curricula, student achievement, and disciplinary treatments.

The Framework and the embedded Tools of Cultural Proficiency are described in detail in Chapter 4. As you proceed through this chapter and then Chapters 2 and 3, you will learn the Tools of Cultural Proficiency:

- Barriers function as default negative core values for embracing students' cultures as deficits. Cross (1989) identified barriers to be the following: systemic forms of oppression, a sense of privilege and entitlement, resistance to change, and unawareness of the need to adapt in ways that serves all students in our schools and school districts.

- The nine Guiding Principles of Cultural Proficiency inform intentional development of core values that shape your behavior and actions as an educator. Additionally, the Guiding Principles might be used to inform development of core values that guide your school and school district's policies and practices in meeting the educational needs of students from diverse cultural communities.
- The Six-Point Continuum represents unhealthy and healthy educator values and behaviors as well as school policies and practices. The deficit-laden barriers foster Cultural Destructiveness, Cultural Incapacity, and Cultural Blindness. Cultural Precompetence, Cultural Competence, and Cultural Proficiency are informed by the Guiding Principles.
- The five Essential Elements of Cultural Competence, informed by the Guiding Principles, are expressed as action words to lead your personal behavior and your school's policies and practices.

Stipulation

Before proceeding too deeply into describing challenges and opportunities that we face as a profession, let alone as a country, I'll make an important stipulation. The rancor and vituperation that have surfaced before and since the 2016 general election are not new. No, in fact the anger and viciousness that gives rise to bigotry is an American tradition that surfaces every few years as an unfortunate, cyclical part of our history. I repeat this observation throughout this book and I provide examples of change and the impact of change on some cultural groups. However, what might be unique in our current cycle of anger and viciousness is its link to the modern national election cycle and its aftermath. Irrespective of how people voted or the extent to which the citizenry aligned with the Republican or the Democratic candidate, the 2016 election cycle might long be noted for the unseemly face-to-face personal attacks, for groups of people maligned due to their cultural identity, and for explicit sexual and gender references not often found in public discourse. We educators are left to explain negative models of adult behavior to our students and, at times, to interrupt when we find our students merely repeating what they heard from high-profile political figures. In this realm of social media, it takes only moments for youths to hear and repeat ugly invectives that they, in turn, hurl toward those who are different from themselves. The consequence of this can be a student discipline issue that consumes the attention and energy of educators.

Hostility toward people due to their cultural identity is an unfortunate and recurring theme in our country's history. Yet, I believe with all my heart, it is not necessary for us to be burdened by history. Informed, yes; burdened, no! I further believe it is our responsibility to learn from past failures and successes. Now more than any other time in our history we are better equipped to respond to issues of divisiveness.

The modern push for educational civil rights began with the landmark 1954 *Brown v. Board of Education of Topeka* U.S. Supreme Court decision. The *Brown* decision created a historical watershed that accelerated the process of separating us from our country's apartheid past. Segregation in its many forms was practiced or condoned across our country. *Brown* essentially outlawed segregation and spawned a generation of efforts to comply with the Supreme Court's orders. Legislative and executive mandates that followed the *Brown* decision fostered nationwide compliance endeavors, some of which were successful and many of which were effectively resisted.

During the 1970s I served as a desegregation specialist for two school districts that were voluntarily desegregating. In both districts, local pressures to provide equitable educational opportunities had been brought to the attention of the U.S. Office for Civil Rights who nudged along the voluntary nature of the desegregation process. In each community were people who were strongly supportive of desegregation as well as those who were strongly opposed to desegregation in any form.

The role as desegregation specialist provided my first time to hear the noise of dissension associated with issues of equity in schools. I have no doubt now that the noise had always been there. I just couldn't hear it— mostly, I suppose, because I didn't have to. Given that I was not a direct target of inequitable behaviors and practices, it was easy to not hear the noise of anger, hate, or discrimination.

Children of color were marginalized in those school districts in ways that should not have been acceptable at any point of our history— certainly not today. Issues of inequity persist in our schools in the form of achievement disparities, disproportionate suspensions and expulsions of students of color, and lack of achieving diverse curricula inclusive of all cultures or curricula that accurately reflect the clashes of culture throughout our history.

The climate arising from the current noise presents unhealthy environments for all of our students. News reports tell of students in a cafeteria chanting, "Build the wall," instances of bullying and hate crimes on campuses, and educators edgy over politically infused dissension. In these intense and tense situations, many educators fear explosive situations that they feel ill equipped to handle. It is our responsibility to be aware of negative discourse among national figures and be ready to respond in ways that ensure civility in our schools. Furthermore, we must model a civility that addresses persistent inequities, not the genteel comity that results in holding hands and having a *kumbaya* moment. Feel-good moments are short term and rarely lead to systemic changes in behavior or policy intended to better serve our students.

TECHNICAL AND ADAPTIVE CHANGE

Schools across the country are accustomed to change efforts. Change initiatives range from technical changes that involve doing things differently to adaptive change that involves thinking differently (Heifetz, 1994). Early school desegregation efforts can be characterized as being focused on technical solutions of student and teacher school assignments in addressing issues of school and community segregation. Title IV of the 1964 Civil Rights Act, the Emergency School Aid Act, and policies flowing from early legislation intended to support school districts in their desegregation initiatives provided fiscal resources for use in adapting to schools' professional development and curricular development needs.

Resistance from some educators and community members too often confined school desegregation efforts to a technical solution of assigning students and faculty in ways that created racial balance. I recall serving as a consultant with a large school district in which an urban predominately African American school was paired with a suburban predominately white school. Irrespective of the plan, no white children traveled to the African American community and the African American students who traveled to the suburban school were assigned to classes of almost all African American students. Clearly such events are illustrations of a technical response to a court order to desegregate that led to active resistance to the spirit if not the word of the court order. Subsequent to desegregation efforts, national attention continued to focus on inequities and led to court decisions such as *Lau v. Nichols* (1974) that continued the pressure on schools to provide educational opportunities for historically marginalized students.

Thankfully, in the mid 1990s Ray, Kikanza, and I were led to Cross's (1989) Cultural Competence work and, after deep consideration, embraced its Tools of Cultural Proficiency as an adaptive approach for leading educators and their schools to turn inward and reflect on their own values and behaviors and, in turn, their schools' policies and practices that hinder and/or facilitate student learning.

In fewer than sixty years our country has removed legal sanctions for segregation and now requires evidence of effective education in our schools. Though long overdue, moving from segregation to the public expectation for educational quality is a monumental step in the right direction. Even with its many limitations, the 2002 reauthorization of the Elementary and Secondary Education Act, known as No Child Left Behind (NCLB), had the silver lining of making the achievement gap public and, thereby, holding schools accountable for the education of all students.

The most casual student of our nation's history knows examples of divisive and conflictive political discourse in which opposing views and interests are part of the historical fabric of this nation. From its beginnings slavery had detractors and resistors. The Westward Expansion and the attendant removal of Native Americans from tribal lands were and continue to be met with resistance throughout society. The women's movement has roots deep in our history. Jim Crow was our country's most visible legal segregation and was institutionalized in the Southern states. Legalized segregation was also alive and well throughout the North, often practiced in what were called "sundown towns" (Loewen, 1995). People of conscience spoke fiercely against all manifestations of institutional racism and resisted segregation in all forms. Homosexuality was criminalized and gave rise to the modern lesbian, gay, bisexual, and transgender (LGBT) movement (Miller, 2006). Even with our history of resistance, our country's legacy of segregation, discrimination, and related violence continues to surface in the form of hate speech, vandalism and graffiti, and physical assaults.

Hostility toward historically marginalized groups arising from the noise surrounding the 2016 general election and its aftermath is not ahistorical. Even within competing political narratives, racial, ethnic, gender, and social class tension has been and continues as a subtext of our national story—often minimized, trivialized, and shoved to the side as if they were aberrant footnotes to a master narrative of an often-mythologized American Exceptionalism.[1]

National attention for addressing educational inequities has progressed from compliance-based technical approaches to more systemic adaptive approaches, such as abandoning pacing guides in favor of differentiating instruction, thankfully, represents a paradigmatic shift in thinking about educating all students in an inclusive manner. The goal posts have moved from simple compliance to a requirement for demonstrated results.

Though uneven, there are schools and school districts across the country demonstrating a willingness and capability to educate all students. My perspective as a teacher of history leads me to believe and know that the divisive rhetoric that too often had race, gender, and religiously bigoted tones surrounding the 2016 general election and its aftermath, though real and really ugly, cannot define us today as we move forward to tomorrow.

REFLECTION

How do you react to the information in this section? In what ways do you see technical and adaptive changes as evidence of inclusivity in your

---

1. It is my belief that profound American Exceptionalism is not embodied in heroic deeds or land possessed, but rather resides in our country's ability to evolve in being inclusive, which is leading us to become a democracy that can be.

school or school district? Please use the space below to record your thinking.

_____

_____

_____

EXPRESSIONS OF BIGOTRY
CAN BE MOTIVATIONAL

The subtitle to this section seems a bit counterintuitive, does it not? At first glance, it doesn't seem natural to experience "bigotry" and "motivational" in the same sentence. Bigotry is always with us, and is seemingly part of the human condition. Bigotry surfaces underlying negative values expressed toward others. Rather than ignoring bigotry, let's confront and transform bigoted behavior.

The noise that has surfaced from the 2016 election cycle can be viewed as providing the opportunity to make the future better for everyone, with particular emphasis on historically marginalized students and their communities. Educators must step forward in ways that recognizes bigoted behavior is the signal to ensure core values and attendant policies and practices that embrace marginalized people's cultures as assets.

As a student of history, I am aware of bigotry in its many manifestations. Bigotry is biased behavior expressed toward others' racial, gender, social class, religious, and sexual orientation groups; it is evidenced throughout human history and from all corners of our planet. Also, as a student of history I am aware that many religious and philosophical movements hold core values that oppose bigotry in its many manifestations. My Methodist upbringing taught me to "do unto others as I would have them do unto me." Let me be clear: I am not advocating for people who are targets of hate and bigotry to turn the other cheek. No, I am appealing for those of us who are the leaders in our schools to use moments and events of bigotry as launch pads for developing schools and school systems that demonstrably express value for equity and structures that foster a value for inclusion. We must make a commitment to speak and act out against bigotry, and to developing schools and school systems that focus on educating all students with focus on equitable access and outcomes.

I have learned that when bigotry surfaces, whether in the form of hate speech, graffiti, or lowered expectations toward students of color, those events can be used to pivot toward opportunity. Informed and skilled leaders, both nonformal and formal leaders, recognize that displays of bias and oppression can be handled in at least two ways: to address the situation at hand as a one-time event and otherwise ignore underlying influences, or to address the situation in ways that precludes or minimizes the recurrence of negative attitudes and behaviors. Making such a pivot is not easy but can be performed by educators who value inclusive, socially just educational environments. Intentional inclusivity is best summarized by a phrase that recurs in this book and is rightfully attributed to the late Asa Hilliard (1991) as a test of our will and skill (p. 31). What Hilliard describes as a test of our will might best be traced back to gaps in knowledge about unpleasant chapters of our country's history that are too often missing from mainstream history books.

Our national heritage includes grand individual and national accomplishments as well as tragic events and systems that continue to sustain traditions of inequity. Inequities born of systemic racism, ethnocentrism, sexism, heterosexism, religious intolerance, and social class divisiveness are as much a part of our national heritage as are the economic benefits of the Westward Expansion and the Industrial Revolution, both of which are thoroughly covered in school curricula. Throughout our history, periods of repression, sometimes brief and too often protracted, have witnessed amazing brutality that led to loss of life, loss of human and civic rights, loss of property, and marginalization from mainstream political and economic processes. The American playwright Tony Kushner in *Angels in America* (2013) states it beautifully: "In this world there is a kind of painful progress." When one takes a long view through these historical periods, one can detect progress; in fact, substantial progress, though uneven, is under way. It is the uneven-ness that attracts our attention now. Our work—our journey—is not nearly complete.

A very important note needs to be made when observing and communicating about progress. Progress toward equitable access and outcomes is easiest to see when one is a member of dominant groups that have benefited from social progress. Keep this notion in mind as you continue reading for it might shape your own learning and foster deep professional learning when in dialogue with colleagues.

REFLECTION

Bigotry. It is a curious word, is it not? Definitely not a word of endearment. In thinking about bigotry as presented, what is occurring for you? What might be your thoughts or feelings? Please use the space below to record your thinking.

_____

_____

_____

DESIGN OF THIS BOOK

You might have noticed that the title for this book includes the word "manifesto." My decision to refer to this work as a manifesto stems from the initial conversation about this book with Dan Alpert, my Corwin colleague and editor who I mentioned in the introduction. As we discussed this book as a concept, Dan used "manifesto" to describe many educators' need for socially just goals and actions as the education community strives to meet the academic needs of our diverse and ever-changing schools' demography amidst the emergent noise from the 2016 election cycle and its aftermath.

I continue to use the word "manifesto" in terms of a statement of policy that might inform our actions as educators. I purposefully and intentionally connect my thinking to the Cultural Proficiency Framework. A key feature of the Framework is that it guides educators to engage in an inside-out process of continuous improvement. The highly respected professional development organization Learning Forward characterizes our educator role as one of being engaged in continuous professional learning and development. Educators in the twenty-first century must be engaged in ongoing learning about the knowledge of our craft and maturation in the skills and attitudes in delivering our craft (Lindsey, Lindsey, Hord, & Von Frank, 2016).

The inside-out process of learning implicit with Cultural Proficiency functions at two levels where we use our time-honored twin communication skills of reflection and dialogue. These processes enable us to be increasingly effective in working with colleagues and students who are culturally different from ourselves. The intentional and mindful use of reflection and dialogic processes lead us to examine our values and behaviors and our school's/district's policies and practices to ensure they meet the educational needs of our students. To that end, the design of this book, or manifesto, is intended to be interactive. You are provided opportunities to think and reflect—or, to put it another way—to think about your thinking.

My intent is for you and me to think together and in doing so to continue to guide us, our profession, and our country in meeting the educational needs and aspirations of all students.

CHAPTER 2

A Brief History of Inequity and Equity: A Tsunami Warning

Early in my career I learned the extent to which inequity is ingrained in our society. I observed the demographic profiles of students in my classes and witnessed the process of sorting students into high- and low-ability classes. Though many fellow educators opined that grouping or tracking was flexible, rarely were students moved up to more-challenging courses.

In pursuing my master's degree at the University of Illinois, my first course focused on a large part of this country's history that had been invisible to me. Throughout my career as a student—from sixth grade to eighth grade to eleventh grade, and then to the university classroom—I completed successfully at least four required courses in U.S. history. Even though the depth of content progressed, there was similarity among the courses. Yes, of course there was overlap, and yet each course deepened my knowledge and appreciation of the development of the United States of America! Those courses, each taught by dedicated and learned instructors, were almost totally devoid of women or people of color in terms of their contributions to the development of our republic. My master's degree program at the University of Illinois included a course titled Negro American History. It was disturbing. It was disturbing because I learned information about people and events of our history as if I was enrolled in a course about a United States that was different from the one I had grown up in. I was experiencing an altered state of reality! The course was about events and experiences and perspectives to which I had been oblivious. The course was disturbing in that it stirred my ignorance, naïveté, and complacency in ways I could not have predicted. I have often wondered, if I had known the disruption this one course caused me, would I have enrolled? The course was fabulous, the professor was highly effective, and my view of myself as an educator shifted to never be the same again. I could no longer maintain my levels of not knowing and live with myself personally or professionally. I was beginning to understand the moral part of being an educator.

> **Lesson Learned #1: The failure to have curriculum and instruction that portrays our history in authentic ways and represents our society inclusively illustrates a form of educational malpractice that ill equips educators and our students to function effectively in our country.**

Michael Fullan's important work, *The Moral Imperative of Educational Leadership* (2003), served to crystallize my thinking and prompted me to reflect on my key teacher and administrator experiences that supported my evolution as a social justice educator. As an administrator, I codirected school desegregation programs in two school districts—one in Illinois and one in Ohio. Reading Fullan's book guided me to reflect on those leadership experiences and to see that too often the work of school desegregation was compliance based. At the time I was coleading the work of desegregating our districts' schools, we referred to our activities as reform efforts. Our social and political context was the 1960s and 1970s with the emergence of the modern civil rights movement. Even though our district and school programs had significant professional development components intended to address educators' and schools' curriculum and instruction, the primary focus was on the physical desegregation of school sites and ensuring that faculties and student bodies were racially mixed. Students were being reassigned to new schools, but too often educator and community members' hearts and minds were not changing about where students belonged within the schools' academic and cocurricular experiences.

Nationally, local school desegregation efforts were designed and implemented in response to judicial and legislative mandates. Too often students' educational needs were secondary to responding to legal and quasi-legal initiatives. I don't argue with the necessity to push or otherwise motivate some communities and school districts to dismantle segregated practices, only that desegregation was not the desired end. The desired end was for students to have equitable access and outcomes in their school experiences. Progress in addressing issues of equity and inequity in our schools has been and continues to be uneven. Uneven progress continues as a historical disservice to students of color. The challenges to equitable opportunities and outcomes are deeply rooted in the nation's fabric and remain with us today.

Whatever the history—forty years ago or yesterday—the goal of witnessing high academic achievement/outcomes by all students in our schools, whether public, private, or religious affiliates, must be our profession's commitment to society.

Desegregation mandates were the initial step for most school districts across the country to even begin addressing issues of inequity. Gradually, it became apparent that desegregation efforts could be a foundation on which to build. Desegregation efforts provided data that African American students could learn when provided accessible school resources. This learning upended the dominant narrative that too often painted pictures of African American students' curricular deficits and deficiencies. The problem was not the students or their home cultures.

In my reflective search for direction, Fullan guided me to recognize and understand the need, and the appropriateness, of appealing to educators beyond the mandate. We needed to appeal to our higher sense of moral purpose. The issues that impede student access and achievement have not changed materially in the past two generations. However, today we have new, and even more powerful resources. Today we have readily available data that identifies inequities. We have schools and school districts addressing achievement disparities in systemic ways and making steady, sometimes remarkable, progress. We have schools and school districts whose educators hold continuous professional development and learning in high esteem. It is my experience that when educators are involved in professional development and learning that utilizes a growth mindset, they are, in turn, equipped to be more effective and inclusive in working with diverse student populations. Furthermore, it is my experience that each of us is on a continuous learning continuum that is not always a linear learning process.

CYCLES OF DISRUPTION AS LEVERS FOR CHANGE: A TSUNAMI WARNING

People who live in areas prone to tornadoes, hurricanes, volcanoes, or earthquakes know that after one event, they begin planning for the next event. It might arrive tomorrow, next month, or in ten years, but they know it will come. As previously indicated, our country experiences cycles of disruption at about thirty-year intervals. We learn over time to install a tornado shelter to reduce the likelihood of destruction next time. What are we learning from the noise rising from the 2016 election cycle and equity in our schools?

My concern relates to the current expressions of anger, fear, and resistance that surfaced around the 2016 primary and general elections and their aftermath. The underlying dynamics of racism, sexism, heterosexism, and class divisions are with us again. Historically the tensions and reactions to systemic oppression have erupted in cyclical historical patterns, often triggered by single events such as a shooting. Other times catalytic events emerge more slowly. The charged language used by candidates and their supporters in the 2016 general election have contributed to raised levels of noise. Even in the context of competing forces we continue to make progress and, yes, there is still much progress to be made. We also know the dynamics of resistance to change persist and are expressed as hate speech, hostile graffiti, and bullying. Whatever is happening in the general society will spill over into our schools (e.g., bullying and other physical assaults, bomb threats).

Efforts to push back against diversity and inclusivity, let alone the absence of decorum, can be recognized as our profession's seismic or tsunami warning, and can be embraced as an opportunity to confront intolerance and build equitable educational structures. Understanding the systemic nature of inequity is an important step in preparing ourselves to successfully educate children and youths from all demographic groups in our society.

INEQUITIES ARE ON OUR DOORSTEPS FOR US TO ADDRESS

Learning and understanding the historic context of equity in our society, schools, and classrooms can be liberating for some educators. Educators release nervous energy when they recognize that they did not cause the social and educational inequities that lead to disproportional assignment of students of color to special education classes; students of color being suspended and expelled numbers disproportional to their numbers in the school population; and students of color being underrepresented in advance placement and similar advanced courses. However, the inequities are ours to address. Historical forces delivered inequities to our doorstep.

Leading our schools and school districts to higher levels of educator effectiveness and student achievement involves understanding historical inequities. Comprehending historical and societal inequities is instrumental to developing an understanding for the "why" and "how" of equitable practices. To understand equity, we probe to determine what inequities might exist in our individual practice. Once we make a commitment to our personal journey in understanding our assumptions, we are well suited to probe the equity profiles of our school's or school district's policy development and implementation of educational practices. In understanding historical context, the choice is ours to become equitable educators and schools (Lindsey, Roberts, CampbellJones, 2013). Identifying unrecognized or unacknowledged inequities in our classroom or school is a basic first step in devising equitable educational practice.

The risk in proposing discussions of how our country's heritage of inequity continues to affect today's schooling is often met with disbelief and is dismissed with comments like, "That was then, this is now," or "All it takes is effort." The fact that inequity was codified into the U.S. Constitution and that social and political inequities were consistent with the times in the late eighteenth century is important information. Only property-owning white males were guaranteed rights in our Constitution. Neither women, nor African Americans, nor First Nations people, nor non-landowners were participating citizens in the early phases of our country. Yet women and people of color were working and participating in the nation's growth as if they were invisible. Parallel and often overlapping gender and racial discrimination existed together with social stratification in which low-income white men were marginalized from being full-fledged members of society. White men had more social mobility than women or people of color, but also knew their "place" or role in society. An advantage they inherited, in most cases, was not being on the lowest rung of the socioeconomic ladder. In fact, during the European migrations of the late eighteenth and throughout the nineteenth centuries, migrants often stepped up into an emerging middle class due to their advantage of being white and being able to participate in the political and economic functions of society. The opportunity to ascend into the middle class does not detract from their hard work, sacrifices, or accomplishments. The distinction is that no matter how hard women and people of color strived, the doors were shut or, at best, opened only slightly.

Those Americans who were privileged by virtue of their skin color, gender, or socioeconomic status participated in the political, economic, and social development of our nascent republic. Again, the U.S. Constitution did not provide basic rights to *all* people—only to property owners, which at that time were white men. Significant illustrations of our country having codified historical inequities are

- Chattel. Slaves figured into the Constitution as a way to balance the more heavily populated northern states with southern states where white people were far fewer. The 3/5 Compromise, cemented into the U.S. Constitution, counted slaves as 3/5 of a person for purposes of apportionment in the U.S. House of Representatives and to provide southern states more representatives. That slaves were considered property is clearly represented in this most important of national treasures, the U. S. Constitution.
- Women's Suffrage. Women could not vote in federal elections until 1920 with the passage of the 19th Amendment.
- First Nations People. Aboriginal people native to the Americas were systematically denied basic rights of citizenship.

All is not lost. Depressing as it is, there are glimmers of hope. Women, people of color, and sometimes their white male allies throughout our nation's history pressed to change the social contract. Passivity was not a widespread norm. Progress made since the signing of the U.S. Constitution in 1787 is due to those who could see the promise of a new and inclusive version of democracy. Countless faceless people have used a variety of legal, political, and economic avenues to press for changes in society. Widely recognized movements were the women's suffrage movement formalized in the mid-nineteenth century and the abolitionist movement that surfaced in the late eighteenth century. However, engrained resistance accompanied efforts for equal rights from day one and continues to this day.

THE SILVER LINING OF EQUITY IN OUR FOUNDING DOCUMENTS

In direct contrast to the initial exclusion and marginalization of women and people of color, our founding fathers provided unintended gifts of equity in the founding documents. It is doubtful the founding fathers intended to serve the goals of equity and social justice in the manner intended today, but they included amendatory change processes that allowed our country to evolve in ways not consistent in the realities of late-eighteenth-century North America.

The long-range equity legacy of the U.S. Constitution might be found in its amendment process and the checks and balances system among the three branches of government that continue to serve our evolving society. Using these levers of power, twentieth-century education began responding to the educational needs of citizens from all demographic groups present in our country that continues into this century.

The twentieth century was witness to the branches of the federal government responding to educational inequities through concerted actions. Most prominently might be the 1954 U.S. Supreme Court decision where, in a 9–0 vote, *Brown vs. Board of Education of Topeka* ended legalized segregation then prevalent throughout the country. Contrary to popular knowledge, schools were segregated and inherently unequal across the country not only in the southern states. In 1965 the Elementary and Secondary Education Act and Head Start were far-reaching efforts in President Johnson's War on Poverty to address inequitable school funding and mechanisms to address achievement gaps and promote highly successful compensatory education programs. Then, in 1974, the U.S. Supreme Court in *Lau v. Nichols* expanded the rights of English-learning students. No longer could students be denied education because of their primary language.

> **Lesson Learned #2: People not granted citizenship status at the beginning of our country's history had to be amended into society, and the process of involvement has been and continues to be arduous.**[1]

In the late nineteenth century and throughout the twentieth century basic political rights, not initially granted to all people, were gradually expanded to be increasingly inclusive. We acknowledge numerous success stories throughout this period, and we realize much more work needs to be done for more people to enjoy success. Many African American, Latino, Aboriginal First Nations, Asian Pacific Islander, and low socioeconomic community success stories seem elusive or, when realized, are invisible to dominant society. Beatty (2012) notes that for every illustration of progress, there remain illustrations of regression. This is where our work as educators begins.

As I mentioned earlier, the ferment raised during the 2016 general election and aftermath is certainly not unprecedented. However, as I also indicated, no one said this work would be easy. Today we stand on the shoulders of citizens who kept pressing for change and were guided by the sage words from our Declaration of Independence, "that all men . . . are endowed by their Creator with certain unalienable Rights, that among these are Life, Liberty and the pursuit of Happiness." No, it has not been an easy path to an education system that is inclusive and values diversity.

REFLECTION

Take a few moments to mull over the above review of history. Any new information for you? Any assumptions challenged? What questions arose for you? Please record your responses in the space below.

_____

_____

_____

That is where our work—yours and mine—comes in. It was more than idle curiosity that motivated you to pick up this book. Like me, you are looking for answers. What I have learned is we have lots of very good and appropriate answers, approaches, and strategies.

---

1. I attribute this quote to friend and frequent coauthor, Brenda CampbellJones.

Our tasks are to probe our moral center in ways that allows us

- To learn about our students,
- To learn about our students' communities,
- To confront our and our colleagues' low-level assumptions about our students and their communities when we hear and know of them, and
- To ensure that our schools' policies and practices are crafted and implemented in ways that serve the students we have—not the students we used to have or the students some might wish we had.

REFLECTION

What did you think when you first picked up this book? What are some of your early impressions? Whether or not you are a student of history, most likely you recognize that historical forces have created the many gifts and challenges that we inherit as educators, let alone as citizens. Now that you have read the section above, what thoughts, reactions, feelings, or questions occur for you? Please use the space below to record your thoughts.

_____

_____

_____

_____

MORE ABOUT ACHIEVEMENT GAPS

Span and Rivers's (2012) research revealed that educators studying the achievement gap by comparing African American students to white students in any given year is restrictive and avoids the essential focal point. Their study as educational historians describes the remarkable progress that African American students have made since the 1954 legal dismantling of the apartheid practices of Jim Crow in schools and school districts across the country. The academic gains made by African American students in seventy years to overcome three hundred years of slavery and legalized segregation is remarkable. Compensatory education programs that flowed out of the Elementary and Secondary Education Act and Head Start in 1965 supported our students across demographic racial, ethnic, and socioeconomic lines. Hopefully you and your colleagues will be motivated to conduct similar studies that center on longitudinal achievement patterns of Latino, Aboriginal First Nations, and Asian Pacific Islander student groups.

Longitudinal, intergenerational studies do not replace year-over-year comparisons, but can be used to complement annual achievement assessments such as the NAEP. An unfortunate by-product of our assessment movement over the past generation has been use of assessments to reinforce the belief that our most vulnerable students are disadvantaged. In reality, these students and their predecessors have too often been subjected to programs not designed to meet their needs and often had them tracked in low-level unchallenging courses throughout their K–12 careers. NAEP has been disaggregating assessment data since 1971 and too often the data have served to reinforce negative stereotypes instead of designing or selecting and implementing programs that would meet students' access and academic needs. In reality, the achievement gap has been well documented for more than forty years but not well acknowledged within our profession. The data have been available and we too often chose not to examine it critically in ways that betrayed our assumptions about our students. It is not an exaggeration to proclaim that an educational debt is owed to racial and ethnic communities with long histories of having been targeted by legalized discrimination. Take a moment and turn back to Lesson Learned #2 to refresh your thinking about our levels of responsibility.

This is not easy work. If it were, I wouldn't be writing this book and you would not be seeking resources to support your efforts at continuous improvement. We must focus on making substantive changes in a profession that seeks immediate solutions.

THE MYTH OF FAILING PUBLIC SCHOOLS

The students for whom our schools were designed are generally doing well. Students whose demographic counterparts were doing well in the 1960s and 1970s are doing as well if not better now in the twenty-first century. The latter half of the twentieth century was witness to an expansion of demographic groups attending high school owing to state-level requirements for compulsory education. Though successes are many, the challenges and uneven progress across demographic groups are evident.

In the context of changing school demography, school reform of the latter part of the twentieth century into the twenty-first century revealed a demographic profile of more students from lower socioeconomic groups attending and graduating from high school. Reform measures that involved a more diverse student population often failed to consider students' cultures as assets; rather, they considered them to be disadvantages to be corrected. This disadvantage status often led to students being placed into remedial courses from which it was difficult to exit or within which it was difficult to be able to perform well on standardized tests (Borrero, Yeh, Crivir, Suda, 2012; Lindsey, Karns, Myatt, 2010).

The phrase "school reform" is laden with problems that often undercut any intended good outcomes. To reform implies a need to improve and sends the message, intended or otherwise, that current practice is ineffective. Quite often the people or schools being reformed don't see a need to change and are content with current practice. The Cultural Proficiency Framework represents a growth mindset in which educators are engaged in ongoing professional development and learning in which it is assumed that students can learn; in turn, we have the capacity to learn to use students' cultures as assets on which to construct their educational experiences.

Our national experience with school desegregation sent a very clear message to society that the education of African American students was not equal in segregated settings. As the nation's schools mobilized to respond to legislative and judicial mandates for compliance, massive resistance occurred, initially in Southern states as they were first mandated to desegregate. By the 1970s resistance to desegregation had spread throughout our country. While there are many success stories related to school desegregation or integration, those success stories have not served to advance equity on a national basis.

Many of our schools exert great effort in successfully educating African American students. When not successful, however, the default position too often is the belief that schools are being blamed unfairly for the failure of society to correct the inequities resulting from three centuries of the lingering effects of slavery and Jim Crow practices. Increasingly, as national consciousness was being raised about racial disparities, our profession began to focus on related systemic inequities affecting female students, English learning students, special need students, and Native American or First Nations students.

Unfortunately, in my view, the perceived "failure" of public schools to successfully address these systemic, societal issues in a generation or two is a rallying cry for "reforming" public education in ways that further segregate those most vulnerable. I go so far as to state that many of the detractors to public education are more focused on further isolating low-income students and students of color than they are in facing the complex task of educating all students, whether they are in integrated or racially isolated school settings.

The 1954 U.S. Supreme Court decision, *Brown v. Board of Education of Topeka,* ushered in an era of multiple school reform movements that sought to prepare students for democratic citizenship (a public purpose) and to give students an equal opportunity for social mobility (a private goal) (Spencer, 2013).

It is incumbent on our profession to embrace and commit to longitudinal continuous improvement of all students. Span and Rivers (2012) discovered that educators' collective mindset of demographic groups being capable of high academic success could be realized. The good news is that it is never too late for all students to experience success in our schools, irrespective of demographic composition. Student success will come when educators hold a commitment to believing our students are capable of learning at high levels and that we are capable of teaching all students. Year-over-year comparisons might have some benefits, but not when those data are used to stigmatize demographic groups of students as being disadvantaged when, truth be told, their progress given generational and systemic inequities is remarkable.

SCHOOL REFORM FROM 1980s TO PRESENT

The 1980s witnessed a pivotal turning point in which economic competition among the countries of the world expanded in unprecedented ways. Suddenly, the United States was faced with a need for workers who could fulfill the technology demands of the new workforce; the industrial factory model was dead, buried, finished—yet the factory model of schools sorting and selecting students remains alive and well! The goals of public schools shifted from preparing students for democratic citizenship to preparing them to work in fast-paced, nimble companies that were competing with comparatively low-wage foreign workforces and even in high-tech industries. The movement to cultivate twenty-first-century skills that emerged in the late 1990s had its greatest impact on affluent predominately white communities. It seems the Common Core Standards are a potentially promising step given the emphasis placed on college and career readiness.

Concurrently, as national and competing international economies were rapidly evolving and becoming more technology based, opposition to court-mandated school reform efforts led to institutional changes, especially the rise of state legislative and executive activity and a strong ethos of local control. Above all, these changes went hand in hand with a concept of equality that changed in three ways:

- From the protection of rights to the reform of whole school systems that were thought to have produced inequalities in the first place;
- From equality of inputs (funding, access to schools and to programs) to an emphasis on educational outcomes as measured by standardized tests; and
- From sameness to the notion that all students should receive at least an *adequate* education, defined in relation to standards (Spencer, 2013; Superfine, 2013).

These views of equity-fostered reforms intended to change what was wrong with students and/or schools in a matter of a few years. When results were not forthcoming, once again, some politicians and prominent business leaders have stridently declared the failure of public schools. My interest is not to weigh the relative merits of these initiatives but to point out that generational issues are not met with overnight change requirements to produce easily documentable results to be touted widely. Illustrations of current reform efforts that have merit and application to our profession but have been misused, in my opinion, to focus on providing near-term student academic gains include

- Standards-based reform and accountability policies, NCLB, and benefits of demographic data (i.e., not subgroup);
- School choice and vouchers; and
- More-robust forms of teacher evaluation (Spencer, 2013) and administrator evaluation (California Department of Education, 2013).

GOING DEEPER

Take a few moments and think about your thinking. What is occurring for you? In what ways does the information in this chapter inform your thinking? In what ways does the chapter challenge your thinking? What new questions do you have that you might not have had before reading this chapter? Think about your own school or school district. To what extent do you recognize illustrations of inequity and equity? What are some examples? What questions do you have about your classroom or school? Please use the space below to record your thinking.

_____

_____

_____

_____

DIALOGIC ACTIVITY

This activity provides opportunity to begin profound cultural change for you, your school, and your school district. Engage colleagues in dialogue to reach shared understanding of a school culture in support of all learners performing at levels higher than ever before. What might be some existing mindsets in your school or school district to be scrutinized and confronted? In what ways are group members willing to engage reflection about their own values and behaviors in working with cultural groups different from yours? What would you risk in reflecting on your values and behaviors? What is the risk for your students if you choose not to do so? For transformative change to occur for you and your school, what data are readily available that would paint a picture of your school's ethnic/racial, gender, and socioeconomic diversity? What is your prediction of the picture as it represents student access to higher-level thinking experiences, to creative thinking/writing, and to academic success? Use the space below to record your current thinking. Your thoughtful reflection and dialogue about these questions will deepen the value and use of this book as you continue to read and think deeply about your role as an educator.

_____

_____

_____

_____

CHAPTER 3

History and Hope for Changing Schools

EDUCATION LANGUAGE AND THE POWER OF "WHY?"

The previous chapter provided a critical look at school reform efforts from the 1980s up to the present. Just how often have you heard terms such as "reform," "education reform," or "transform"? In my fifty-plus years as an educator who aspires to be inclusive and socially just in my actions, I have learned that we have inherited a coded language. Intentionally or not, this coded language communicates to many in our profession and the diverse communities we serve that school was not designed to serve students of color and students from low-income communities in the same way we serve students from predominately middle-class, white communities.

Let's think together for a moment. If we were truly serving the educational needs of all students we would not use terms such as "reform," "education reform," or "transform." What is it exactly that we need to reform? The very use of such terms at times indicates that we are well prepared to serve the educational needs of *some* students. Yet other students aren't well served by our educational systems. Why is it that many of us who enter this profession that is so central to a vibrant democracy are often ill equipped to educate some students? What might we and our schools and school districts be communicating to students and their communities about how we value them?

We are generally effective in communicating to students well served by current practices that they will be successful in our classrooms, in our schools, and in our school districts. Whether conscious or not, we too often communicate to people from historically marginalized communities that somehow their culture, families, and/or neighborhoods are deficit laden—deficits that result in students' lack of success. Rarely do we turn inward to consider that maybe we have to learn new content and skills in order to be successful with children and youths from historically marginalized communities. The distinct message is that these students are different from those being well served by our schools. Most often we communicate exclusion and marginalization through acts of omission:

- We don't know the historical nature of their culture within our country.
- When they are recent immigrants, we don't seem to know the historical, political, or social context of their immigration to this country.
- We don't understand their language.
- We haven't developed the mindset of inclusion, which entails being motivated to learn about them or their culture.

More succinctly, recognizing acts of omission can lead to acknowledging that maybe *we don't even know what we don't know!* Take a moment and read the italicized phrase again. If I don't recognize that my behaviors negatively impact others, how can I learn? Becoming aware of what we don't know guides us to becoming aware of our values and behaviors that intentionally marginalize students. To experience our and our colleagues' growing awareness of acts of omission is a moment of intellectual beauty! Moments of such burgeoning awareness stand in sharp contrast to those in which educators intentionally act from a deficit mindset and openly declare that students from designated cultures or neighborhoods are incapable of learning and are not worthy of high-level curricula or instruction. Aberrant educator behavior that is this blatantly racist or sexist, truthfully, is a matter for the Human Resources (HR) department. However, such HR violations aren't exclusively the domain of supervising administrators; ownership must also be shared among colleagues—teacher to teacher, administrator to administrator, counselor to counselor, etc. Our professional and moral responsibility is to shine the light on fellow educators' unprofessional and discriminatory attitudes and behaviors that are public. We can no longer remain silent as if we agree. We must act in a professional way and counter the negative behaviors with Culturally Proficient practice.

Let's pause for a second. There is an important caveat to consider. The social, political, economic, and educational processes that have resulted in educational inequities are not always of our doing; however, they are ours to address. Which leads me to

> **Lesson Learned #3: While we did not cause racism, sexism, or any form of systemic oppression, the ill effects of those systems are ours to address.**

When you hear colleagues use the terms "reform," "educational reform," or "transform," what comes to mind? Take a few moments and reflect on how those terms are used by you, by your colleagues, and by the larger communities we serve. Use the space below to record your recollections of how the terms are used—context, content, focus, judgment, etc.

_____

_____

_____

_____

Understanding the "why" of educational reform efforts is important. We have become adept as educators in responding to "what" and "how" questions. Schools and school districts across the country have demonstrated repeatedly that they can follow dictates for change and implement almost any educational practice in a short period. We have become masters of responding to the "what" and "how" of learning and implementing new approaches to curricular and instructional practice. This is not to say that we agree with the new practices or the rationale for the changes; it is that we have become adept at following dictates—whether from local, state, or national officials. And, yet, access and achievement gaps persist. The same demographic groups of students are still not as successful in our schools as we would like them to be. Too often the default position for explaining persistent, continuing access and achievement gaps is to regard students' cultural backgrounds as the culprit. Certainly, the gaps couldn't be for our lack of effort!

In truth, most often it is our effort that is misplaced and our energies not used well. My experience is when we embrace our students' cultures as assets; we increase our ability to be successful. A kind of introspection is required here. As evidenced by the campaigning that accompanied the 2016 election cycle, a strong tendency exists to marginalize people from cultures who are different from the mainstream dominant white culture represented in our schools' curriculum and in the demographic profile of our educators.

Let me be clear. There is no need to vilify mainstream dominant white culture or any other culture represented in our schools. I know from personal experience that an educator from any cultural group can be successful educating a student from any cultural group as long as he is willing to examine his assumptions about the student's culture. At the same time, having a diverse faculty and staff sends strong messages of inclusivity and expressions of culture being valued. That pesky "why" question again! I have learned that educators who are willing and able to confront our own assumptions as well as the assumptions built into our schools' policies and practices are poised for success.

TRANSFORMATIVE CHANGE

Our profession's commitment to all students learning at high levels has been a slow, evolving process. Understanding the history and context of educational reform and change equips us in making informed decisions about our ongoing professional learning and guides the professional learning and development of our schools and school districts.

The following section is designed to support you by

- Articulating an understanding of how mindsets shape perception;
- Making summary comments on the evolution of educational reform in the United States;
- Describing the ways in which educational reform and continuous improvement for transformative change inclusive of all demographic groups of students might be similar in definition but might hold very different effects when used in our schools;
- Summarizing the relationship of educational reform to issues of diversity, access, and equity; and
- Differentiating among types of leadership and their relationship to access, equity, and diversity (Lindsey, Kearney, Estrada, Terrell, & Lindsey, 2015, p. 23).

Educators equipped with the skills and knowledge embedded in these five areas of educational change are positioned to address educational gaps in ways that focus on educator learning that embraces students' cultures as assets on which students' educational experiences are to be constructed.

THE ACHIEVEMENT GAP IS NOT NEW

To understand equity, we must know inequity. To fully understand equity is to have deep knowledge of inequities that are both historical and persistent in our society. Parsing the achievement gap entails knowing and understanding the social, political, and economic underpinnings of equity and inequity. Equity and inequity are interconnected.

Exploration of the achievement as a topic from recent U.S. education history provides important context for many of the challenges in our schools today. Though states such as California and Tennessee began disaggregating student achievement data by demographic groups well before NCLB was signed into law by President George W. Bush in 2002, it was

NCLB that brought the achievement gap to the collective national attention as educators and the general public.[1] The relevant question is, "Did the achievement gap exist prior to NCLB or similar state and local initiatives?"

Of course it existed! Those of us who were educators prior to 2002 can attest to the existence of achievement disparities, but we can also confirm our profession's resistance to acknowledging and confronting those disparities. And, as stated in the previous chapter, NAEP results have evidenced the existence of such disparities for more than forty years. In schoolhouses across the country, those who resisted the data stonewalled those educators who tried to inform colleagues' mindsets that were closed to recognizing achievement disparities. In fact, as a profession we became practiced at deflecting concern for achievement by declaring the causes were beyond us. We blamed poverty, neighborhoods, parents, culture, and often all of the above. Of course, poverty and other socioeconomic factors are real-world pressures beyond the control of most schools but they cannot be used to escape our responsibilities to make the time students are on campus as relevant and meaningful as possible.

INTO THE SECOND CENTURY OF EDUCATION REFORM: THE "WHY?" QUESTION

Responding to the underlying "why" question of inclusive and adaptive equity-focused education reform can be transformative for schools and school districts at two levels. First, systemic equity-focused reform efforts are expressly inclusive of all demographic groups of students. Second, educators embrace reform efforts as personal and institutional. Reform efforts are considered as an opportunity and responsibility to create policies and practices that believe students' cultures are assets and not disadvantages.

Culturally Proficient mindsets understand the inequity–equity dynamic to foster equitable practices that expressly include

- Knowledge that education reform has been on a trajectory of continuous improvement since the middle of the nineteenth century;
- Awareness that our democracy has been evolving since the late eighteenth century and that our political, social, and economic evolution has been accompanied by a continuous overarching

---

1. I use the term "demographic group" instead of the more popular term "subgroup" to mitigate the possibility of negative stereotyping. I acknowledge that "subgroup" is a non-pejorative term used by professionals in the assessment community, but we have experienced negative reactions to the term when used with the broader, diverse communities served by our schools and school districts and thereby, respectfully, find "demographic group" to be both descriptive and accurate.

expansion of basic civil rights. That said, it must be acknowledged that though the trajectory has been long-term expansion of civil rights, the journey has been along a zigzag path of advances followed by missteps and some retreats;

- Possession of the knowledge that twenty-first-century schooling is evolving from being a democratization process to being a global competitiveness process, too often positioned as a false dichotomy. Democratization and global competitiveness are mutually reinforcing;

- Uncovering of school-based experiences that show poverty is a conundrum assiduously avoided by government and corporate leaders. Poverty is a condition of society to be addressed; and

- A value for quality professional learning held by, for, and with educators that must be culturally proficient (Lindsey et al., 2015, p. 24).

For education reform to be meaningful, and for associated professional development/learning to be effective, equity, access, and inclusion must be embedded into transformative conceptions of the reform effort. Transformative experiences cause educators to deeply examine their values and beliefs about the cultures of their students and, similarly, to scrutinize their school's policies and practices to ensure inclusivity and equity. Mindsets such as these equip educators to understand deeply equitable education and to tailor all future reforms that emanate from government, the private sector, and our own professional efforts to meet the needs of a demographically diverse student body.

AMIDST THE NOISE IS CLARITY

We have come too far as a nation and as a profession to deny our country's multiculturalism. The hard-fought progress toward human and civil rights of the nineteenth century gave way to the substantial educational equity progress of the twentieth century. The twenty-first century must begin with an acknowledgment that systemic oppression has been a part of our national fabric but that it must be eliminated. Educators along with their schools and school districts are calling for cultural inclusivity that regards cultures as assets; using culturally responsive pedagogy leads to equitable access and outcomes for all demographic groups of our students.

GOING DEEPER

How do you describe the terms "equity" and "transformative change" in your current professional context? What more do you need to learn about the manner in which equity and transformative change are evident in your practice as an educator? In your school's activities? Use the space below to record your responses.

_____

_____

_____

_____

DIALOGIC ACTIVITY

What data would you need to collect to determine where your grade level, department, or school might be along the inequity–equity spectrum? How would you initiate such an activity? Who would you involve in analyzing the data? What would you hope to do with the data?

_____

_____

_____

_____

PART II

Listening for Clarity

Do we have the will to educate all children?

—Asa Hilliard (1991, p. 36)

In Chapter 4 I begin with an overview of the Cultural Proficiency Framework, an overarching model that describes the purpose and function of each of the Tools of Cultural Proficiency. Chapter 5 explores some of the recurring barriers to equity and access—systems of institutional oppression, a sense of privilege and entitlement, resistance to change, and unawareness of the need to adapt. The barriers are presented and discussed in terms familiar to school-based educators. Chapter 6 brings it all together by delving into the operational components of the Cultural Proficiency Framework, the Guiding Principles, and the Essential Elements. Chapter 7 provides opportunity for you to plan next steps.

CHAPTER 4

The Cultural Proficiency Framework

The Cultural Proficiency authors implore school leaders to engage *long-range* transformative initiatives that institute periodic/annual benchmarks focused on continuous improvement for narrowing and closing achievement gaps. Policymakers at local, state, and national levels must ensure long-term equitable funding and access to broadband technology as fundamental for low-income communities and necessary for all students to be ready for college and career choices (Gjaja, Puckett, & Ryder, 2014; Polis & Gibson, 2014).

CULTURALLY PROFICIENT LEADERSHIP

Leadership in the context of our diverse population and our history of systemic inequity must hold equity, access, and inclusion as core values to guide each and every employee of the school and school district. As you proceed in this chapter, you will learn that the Guiding Principles of Cultural Proficiency represent equity, access, and inclusion as central values. For transformative efforts to have long-term impact across student demographic groups, the Cultural Proficiency Framework needs to be embedded into conceptions of school leadership that effectively benefits all students.

Being a culturally proficient educator is to understand the concepts of entitlement and privilege and their relationship to systems of oppression. Racism and other forms of oppression exist only because the dominant group benefits from historical and continued practices that served an often-homogeneous white middle-class clientele. This is not a zero-sum game where if one side gains, another has to lose. Culturally proficient educational leaders shift their thinking to being intentional in understanding both the negative consequences of oppression and the manner in which people have benefited from those same systems. Culturally proficient leaders allocate human and fiscal resources to equitably benefit all students.

As discussed in earlier chapters, reforming and transforming efforts in schools can be viewed as progressing along a spectrum of educational progress. Reform efforts initiated along with desegregation efforts most usually involved selecting more relevant curricular materials and learning and applying new approaches to instruction. Those initial efforts at change have progressed into transformational efforts designed to effectively educate historically marginalized students through confronting power at two levels—the personal authority of the individual educator and the institutional authority of school as a system. Culturally proficient educators embrace their personal power and their schools' institutional authority to address organizational barriers and use their power to transform policies and practices. Weick (1979) contends that organization is a myth and that *most "things" in organizations are actually relationships tied together in systematic fashion* (p. 88). In other words, we invent social organizations through our interactions with one another. The extreme polarities of Cultural Destructiveness and Cultural Proficiency are similarly invented ways of organizing our social interactions, which, once again, is a choice we are to make.

Leadership requires a mindset embracing change as a process to be managed. Shields (2010) describes leadership as a succession of three ever-deepening change processes—transactional, transformational, and transformative. Our schools need and benefit from each type of leadership. Whereas transactional leadership involves reciprocal actions that keep the day-to-day functions of school intact and transformational leadership focuses on organizational effectiveness, it is transformative leadership that values the concepts of equity and access. Equity and access are embraced as moral responsibility in serving the academic and social needs of our diverse communities. Culturally proficient education functions as a moral framework for educational leaders. Culturally proficient leaders ensure that educators' professional learning is focused on the moral imperative of equitable access and outcomes. Culturally Proficient Professional Learning and Culturally Proficient Leadership entail three sides of our moral authority and responsibility:

- Recognizing the dynamics of entitlement and privilege,
- Recognizing that our schools contribute to disparities in achievement, and
- Believing that educators can make choices that positively affect student success (Lindsey et al., 2013).

Cultural Proficiency fosters an inside-out approach to leadership and leaders' commitment to personal and organizational change. Committing to examining our individual values, assumptions, and behaviors naturally extends to a commitment to collaborate with colleagues to examine our school and district policies and practices. Culturally proficient leaders define education in a democracy to be inclusive. Leaders effective in diverse environments necessarily focus on inequity and equity, regardless of who is benefiting from the current policies and practices. **Culturally proficient leaders focus on learning how to serve the academic and social needs of all demographic groups of students, rather than how to change and assimilate members of target groups.** Culturally proficient educational leaders expect challenges from prominent people in the school, the school district, and the community. They operate by remaining centered on the moral value in our work as educators.

> **Lesson Learned #4: All demographic groups of students are capable of high academic achievement and our educators are capable of educating all demographic groups of students.**

Change and change processes are not new to educators. My frequent coauthor, best friend, and wife, Delores Lindsey, when leading professional development sessions with PreK–12 colleagues, often notes, "We in education are not averse to change. In fact, we can adopt a new curriculum, a new bell schedule, or a new tardy system in short order." She continues, "Just give us the What? and How? and we will do it tomorrow." "What" and "how" questions almost always indicate technical changes where we work with current accessible information to solve a problem or dilemma. Then, Delores completes her line of reasoning by noting, "However, our responses to Why? questions guide our schools and us into adaptive changes." Adaptive changes involve changing values, beliefs, and behaviors. Adaptive changes require us to examine our deepest-held assumptions.

Focusing on technical changes gives rise to a pace and rate of change that is often rapid-fire responses to events. Technical responses to educating students from historically marginalized groups of students are responses of "How?" and "What?," and usually are behavior centered. Responses to "What?" and "How?" taken over time, however are slow and uneven. It is when educators are focused on responses to the "Why?" question that drives us beneath educator behavior and educational practice to uncover and understand our underlying assumptions.

It was at Cal State, Los Angeles, with the Regional Desegregation Center that Raymond, Kikanza, and I first noted that the technical changes being implemented in schools often yielded minimal results in accelerating student learning. Too often the implemented changes focused on students and their cultures in ways that regarded them as deficits. This line of thinking appeared intent on remaking these poor unfortunate students fit into the mold of middle-class white kids. Once forced into that mold, students would (presumably) learn. Think about that for a moment. How could students learn when we in education might regard them, their parents/guardians, their cultures, or their neighborhoods as "deficits"? No amount of technical changes can overcome that hurdle. No new reading program. No bussing students to a different school. No language program that functions as speech correction. No amount of urban impact money (i.e., often referred to as "combat pay" to coax educators to work in urban schools). And, certainly not educators who approach students and their community as a missionary experience akin to saving souls could overcome this deficit thinking.

Deficit-focused efforts rarely made measurable, lasting positive impact on the schools or students. Our belief is best exemplified by paraphrasing Pedro Noguera: "There is nothing wrong with the kids!"

As a country and as a profession we continue to struggle in learning how to educate students who are from historically marginalized groups. Seemingly intractable challenges are still in front of us. Across the country are educators transcending technical approaches and embracing adaptive approaches to meeting the needs of these communities. Adaptive processes engage us in examining our behaviors, beliefs, and values regarding the students we have been enlisted to educate.

One such adaptive approach is the Cultural Proficiency Framework, which consists of four interrelated tools to guide educators in articulating inclusive values and behaviors in service of students from diverse communities. Similarly, schools and school districts use the tools within the Framework to guide the development of policies and practices that support students' equitable access to rigorous academic experiences and outcomes.

THE TOOLS OF CULTURAL PROFICIENCY

The Tools of Cultural Proficiency enable you to

- Describe Barriers to Cultural Proficiency you might have experienced or observed that impede cultural proficiency;
- Describe how the Guiding Principles of Cultural Proficiency serve as core values for your personal, professional, and organizational values and behavior;
- Describe unhealthy and healthy values and behaviors and school policies and practices and plot them on the Cultural Proficiency Continuum; and

- Describe and use the five Essential Elements of Cultural Competence as standards for your personal and professional behavior and your school's formal policies and nonformal, prevalent practices.

THE CULTURAL PROFICIENCY CONCEPTUAL FRAMEWORK AS A GUIDE

The Conceptual Framework for Culturally Proficient Practices illustrates the manner in which students' cultures are embraced as assets and form the basis for core values to guide educational leaders. Recognizing and understanding the tension that exists for people and schools in terms of barriers vs. assets prepares you to better serve the students in your classroom, school, and district.

Table 4.1 presents the Conceptual Framework for Culturally Proficient Practices and presents the interrelationships among the four Tools of Cultural Proficiency. The table is best read by starting at the bottom. It might be a bit counter-intuitive to read from the bottom up, so please regard reading in this fashion as a cultural awareness experience. Another consideration is to envision the Framework as metaphor for a structure or building. Most buildings with which I am familiar began with constructing the foundation. With this foundation, you will see two contrasting pillars, one negative and one positive.

BARRIERS VS. CULTURAL ASSETS: THE TENSION FOR CHANGE

The Barriers to Cultural Proficiency and the Guiding Principles (i.e., core values) of Cultural Proficiency are, respectively, the negative and positive pillars of the Framework. As you follow the arrows upward you will note that the Barriers inform the negative side of the Continuum—cultural destructiveness, cultural incapacity, and cultural blindness. At the same time, the Guiding Principles serve to inform the positive side of the Continuum—cultural precompetence, cultural competence, and cultural proficiency. Recognizing and acknowledging the Barriers to Cultural Proficiency is a very important first step to understanding how to overcome resistance to change that resides within us and within our schools. It does not mean that we are bad people. My experience is that when educators probe to understand their embedded assumptions they are almost always able to make positive shifts in working with students and in ensuring school policies and systemic practices are inclusive.

Table 4.1   The Conceptual Framework for Culturally Proficient Practices

The Five Essential Elements of Cultural Competence

Serve as standards for personal, professional values and behaviors as well as organizational policies and practices:

- Assessing Cultural Knowledge
- Valuing Diversity
- Managing the Dynamics of Difference
- Adapting to Diversity
- Institutionalizing Cultural Knowledge

Informs

The Cultural Proficiency Continuum portrays people and organizations who possess the knowledge, skills, and moral bearing to distinguish among healthy and unhealthy practices as represented by different worldviews:

Unhealthy Practices:	Differing Worldviews	*Healthy Practices:*
• Cultural destructiveness		• Cultural precompetence
• Cultural incapacity		• Cultural competence
• Cultural blindness		• Cultural proficiency

Informs   *Informs*

Resolving the tension to do what is socially just within our diverse society leads people and organizations to view selves in terms Unhealthy and Healthy.

Barriers to Cultural Proficiency

Serve as personal, professional, and institutional impediments to moral and just service to a diverse society by

- being resistant to change,
- being unaware of the need to adapt,
- not acknowledging systemic oppression, and
- benefiting from a sense of privilege and entitlement.

Ethical Tension

Guiding Principles of Cultural Proficiency

Provide a moral framework for conducting one's self and organization in an ethical fashion by believing the following:

- Culture is a predominant force in society.
- People are served in varying degrees by the dominant culture,
- People have individual and group identities.
- Diversity within cultures is vast and significant.
- Each cultural group has unique cultural needs.
- The best of both worlds enhances the capacity of all.
- The family, as defined by each culture, is the primary system of support in the education of children.
- School systems must recognize that marginalized populations have to be at least bicultural and that this status creates a distinct set of issues to which the system must be equipped to respond.
- Inherent in cross-cultural interactions are dynamics that must be acknowledged, adjusted to, and accepted.

Table 4.1 lists Barriers to Culturally Proficient attitudes, behaviors, and policies and practices that affect our daily lives and impact educational leaders' decisions (Cross, 1989; Lindsey, Nuri Robins, & Terrell, 2009):

- Being resistant to change,
- Being unaware of the need to adapt,
- Not acknowledging systemic oppression, and
- Benefiting from a sense of privilege and entitlement.

Note the line between the Barriers and the Guiding Principles. That very thin line separates Cultural Blindness and Cultural Precompetence and represents a paradigmatic shifting point where educators have clearly delineated choices:

- In Barriers, to the left of the line, educators are influenced by social forces that give rise to systemic forms of oppression and believe either in cultural deficit theory applied to marginalized communities or, every bit as damaging, accrue often-unacknowledged or -unrecognized benefits from the weight of systemic oppression experienced by marginalized communities. Or,
- To the right of the line, educators mindfully embrace their capacity to successfully educate all students by embracing students' racial, ethnic, gender, socioeconomic, sexual orientation and gender identity, special needs, or faith communities as assets on which to build curriculum and instruction.

Educators' and schools' core values informed by the Guiding Principles of Cultural Proficiency counter the Barriers to Cultural Proficiency. Expressly inclusive core values guide our personal and professional work in ways that marginalized students can be academically and socially successful in schools' programs. Culture is woven into the very fabric of the Guiding Principles and is reflected in our behaviors, policies, and practices. School and school districts' core values must be deeply held beliefs and values. Core values cannot, must not, be lightly considered and must be evident in our everyday practice. The Guiding Principles inform our actions that are Cultural Precompetence, Cultural Competence, and Cultural Proficiency. The Guiding Principles as shown on Table 4.1 are these:

- Culture is a predominant force in society.
- People are served in varying degrees by the dominant culture.
- People have individual and group identities.
- Diversity within cultures is vast and significant.
- Each cultural group has unique cultural needs.
- The best of both worlds enhances the capacity of all.

- The family, as defined by each culture, is the primary system of support in the education of children.
- School systems must recognize that marginalized populations have to be at least bicultural and that this status creates a unique set of issues to which the system must be equipped to respond.
- Inherent in cross-cultural interactions are dynamics that must be acknowledged, adjusted to, and accepted.

TRANSFORMING THE CULTURE OF SCHOOL

Too often the culture most resistant to examining prevalent practices is the organizational culture of school. School improvement initiatives often focus on "change, or needs to be changed" recommendations. Organizational and school culture research indicates schools as organizations have a culture of their own and need leaders who understand and manage that culture in positive ways (Deal & Kennedy, 1982; Fullan, 2003; Schein, 1992, 2010; Wagner et al., 2006).

Experienced and new educators alike acknowledge that change is not easy. Surfacing forces that either block (Barriers) or facilitate (Guiding Principles) student achievement is basic to deep change. Embedding the educational needs of marginalized students into learning and mastering new practices can lead to resistance and responses that range from comments such as, "Most students were doing well so why do we have to change to meet the needs of these students?"

While it might be true that change is not easy, change is inevitable and natural. When properly understood and implemented, change initiatives can focus on the educational needs of traditionally underserved students and, also, benefit all learners in our schools. Culturally proficient practices inclusively focus on struggling learners as well as high-achieving students. Culturally proficient educators create classrooms and school-wide conditions to support all learners achieving at levels higher than before.

All educators must be able to recognize and acknowledge personal and institutional barriers to creating conditions for teaching and learning while advocating for practices that benefit all students, schools, and districts. The Conceptual Framework for Culturally Proficient Practices is a mental model for managing change that can be used to understand and tell our stories in ways that can inform your continued journey to increased effectiveness as an educator (Dilts, 1990, 1994; Lindsey et al., 2009; Senge, 2000).

The Conceptual Framework's four tools equip school leaders with processes for working with colleagues to develop inclusive values and behaviors in their practice and as school communities to develop inclusive policies and practices for their schools and school districts. In Chapter 5 you have the opportunity to begin/continue your "inside-out" process of examining assumptions about cultures different from yours. The chapter covers the tool, Overcoming Barriers to Cultural Proficiency, with particular focus on Resistance to Change.

GOING DEEPER

In thinking about change for you and for your school or school district, what might be some of the barriers that you see? What core values are in place in your school or school district that are inclusive of all students achieving at high levels? Please use the space below to record your thinking.

_____

_____

_____

_____

DIALOGIC ACTIVITY

Engage your colleagues in sharing responses to the question above. Once you have shared your responses, what might be some next steps? Please record responses in the space below.

_____

_____

_____

_____

CHAPTER 5

Resistance to Change: The Anger–Guilt Continuum

Discussions and readings about "-isms" are often challenging for those of us who don't experience the negative effects on a daily or periodic basis. I have no doubt that many among us were a bit perplexed, maybe annoyed, by the allegations of racism, misogyny, Islamophobia, and sexism during the 2016 primary and general elections.

For people who are not targets of the "isms," it can be disquieting to observe, maybe even feel, the reactions of those who do have those experiences. Men who actually hear sexist comments for the first time are often initially disoriented in learning that they had been oblivious for so long. White people who suddenly hear racist comments are often aghast at their own innocence. Actually *hearing* slurs directed to people because of their religious affiliation is disquieting. In each case, the opportunity for developing empathy for other people and their cultural communities is heightened.

Real time empathy is powerful. Empathy that gives rise to members of a dominant group speaking up in moments of injustice is particularly powerful. I have learned from colleagues who are frequent targets of "isms" that they describe empathetic colleagues as people who "get it." As an example, I find that women appreciate men who object to sexist comments and don't wait for the women to respond. The men speak up, not in a way to defend the women, but in a way to let others know the women have spoken or need to be heard. Correspondingly, I have learned that men who are fully aware of their privilege and entitlement also object to sexist comments when the conversation involves only men. Such men demonstrate the link between what they say they value and what they actually do.

SURFACING PRIVILEGE AND ENTITLEMENT

Rarely do I encounter educators who fail, when the question is posed, to acknowledge historical racism or that racism persists in today's society. The same is true when asked about sexism, misogyny, Islamophobia, and other forms of systemic oppression. At that important moment I pose the question, "If we in this room acknowledge that systemic forms of oppression have existed historically and persist today, does it not also make sense that people lose rights and privileges due to being targeted by acts of oppression?" Assent is evident by head nods and hands raised. Next, I pose, "When we agree that people lose rights and privileges due to group membership, does it not also make sense that others accrue those rights and privileges in ways they might not even recognize?" After moments of little movement and blank stares, most often I get nodding assents from some and seemingly stunned silence from others. Awareness is a wonderful thing to experience in self and others! I continue by pointing out that we have just acknowledged the existence of, often unintentional, benefits informed by an awareness that benefits denied to one group do not just disappear. Since an illustration seems appropriate, I continue by asking, "As today's facilitator, if I recognize and involve only the women in group decisions about timing of breaks, does that not marginalize the men in the decision-making process and, also, provide each female group member with a great portion of the decision-making process?" The analogy works and provides an on-ramp to understanding privilege and entitlement.

Conversations about privilege and entitlement often surface emotional reactions that range from anger to guilt. My experiences have been that once educators acknowledge, understand, and own their very real feelings in learning about privilege and entitlement they are ready to begin learning about how to work more effectively with students and communities that are culturally different from theirs. These levels of learning are empowering in that an individual can intentionally and mindfully direct his or her own learning and discover effective ways for working in cross-cultural situations (Cross, 1989; Freire, 1970, 1999). In the following vignette, you will see how two educators at Mystic Elementary School surface their feelings when exploring issues of entitlement and privilege:

Suzanne: You know, I can take this discussion of racism and sexism when the presenters are not so aggressive. Enough is enough!

Clara: What do you mean by "aggressive"?

Suzanne: Well, she just kept presenting information that is so uncomfortable.

Clara: But I do recall her asking about our reactions to the information and what your thoughts were. How is that aggressive? Do you think it would have been different for you if a white male had presented the information?

Suzanne: Why would you ask me if I would have reacted differently had the presenter been a white male?

Clara: Well, as I see it, the presenter was not aggressive toward you. She merely presented ideas that you appeared to find upsetting.

Suzanne: Upsetting? How the hell can you say that?

Clara: Look at yourself right now: You have raised your voice, and you are pointing your finger right in my face. If that is not anger, I don't know what is!

Suzanne: Listen, damn it, I resent people trying to make me feel guilty for something I did not create. I am fully prepared to be accountable for my actions, but I am not going to feel guilty for what "history" or "institutions" have done to anyone!

Educators like Suzanne often become upset when discussing systemic oppression and display anger or guilt or both when topics of privilege and entitlement emerge. Figure 5.1 represents this range of reactions. People who have the ability to listen to the information and not accept the information as anger or guilt are confident they can use the information for constructive purposes. As you can see in Figure 5.1 anger and guilt are at the extreme ends of the continuum and confidence is poised midway.

Educational leaders who choose to remain angry or guilty when initially presented the data of disproportionate low achievement of students of color, for example, contribute to their own paralysis of inaction or inappropriate, actions. In these cases, the educators sometimes express anger in feeling blamed for things from history they did not cause or, conversely, sometimes express guilt that they were not aware of the negative context in which their students lived. In either case, positive fixating at anger and guilt causes no movement to benefit students.

Figure 5.2 indicates that feelings of anger and guilt, although very different at the surface, are similarly dysfunctional and unproductive.

Figure 5.1 Continuum of Reactions to Information About Oppression

Anger	Confidence	Guilt
X ————————————	X ————————————	X

The sense of frustration that arises from feelings of anger and guilt leads to inaction, which does not benefit underachieving students. Even worse, frustration can influence educator's behaviors that lead to schoolwide practices that are counterproductive for underachieving students, such as the "drill and kill" approaches to mathematics and language arts. Many of these approaches and materials surfaced in the wake of accountability measures that flowed in the wake of NCLB. I'll note here that those measures were not dictated by NCLB but were, rather, fumbled attempts to implement facile approaches to accountability.

Conversely, educational leaders who learn about systemic inequities and are able to move from initial feelings that range from anger or guilt to understanding the underlying issues of systemic oppression are poised to take equitable actions with confidence. Educators who are willing to confront their own experiences of anger and guilt can come to awareness that their discomfort might be leading them to deeper learning. They ask themselves, "Why am I bothered? Am I feeling blamed? Am I learning something for the first time?" The educator's confidence is bolstered when grounded in a moral imperative and when the educator is committed to using authentic evidence to select methods and materials deemed effective for each demographic and cultural group of students at the school. Such educators are focused on all students and are naturally curious about what it is as educators they can learn that will affect their educational practice. Teachers, counselors, and administrators viewing the same data learn more about how their educator role supports student learning.

Educators Moving Forward with Confidence. Making conscious, intentional choices is indicative of educators striving to improve their practice. Teacher and counselor effectiveness improves when we work together to select and deliver curricula and teaching practices that meet

Figure 5.2   Functional and Dysfunctional Reactions to Issues of Oppression

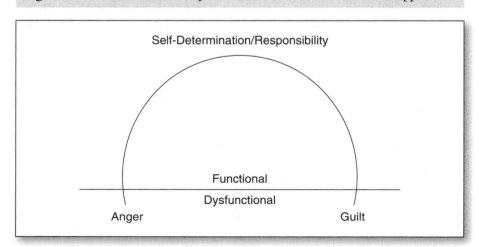

the needs of all demographic groups of students. School administrators' practice is improved through marshaling resources in support of high-quality curricula and instruction. Members of professional organizations and unions improve practice by ensuring that their core values address service to their students. At the policy-making level, improvement of practice involves school board members and district administrators setting and implementing policy that provide access for students from all sectors of the community. Advocating for equity necessitates being proactive and asserting one's needs, opinions, and views. Leading for equity also requires us to take responsibility to facilitate others, particularly those who are silent, in understanding that exploring their assumptions can be an important avenue to new and deeper learning.

What is the difference between those who get stuck in dysfunction and those who are able to move forward with confidence? Think back to the Cultural Proficiency Continuum. The difference is the successful transition in a shift in thinking and disposition from cultural destructiveness, cultural incapacity, or cultural blindness to cultural precompetence and, eventually, cultural competence. The point between these two positions is analogous to what Gladwell (2000) termed the "tipping point." It is that point in time when a shift in thinking occurs. The shift in thinking occurs when the educational leader sees the behaviors of cultural destructiveness, incapacity, and blindness as inauthentic and inappropriate and is willing to shift to the arenas of possibility provided by culturally competent behaviors. The shift in thinking occurs when leaders recognize their stereotypic feelings and reactions and, through processes of reflection and dialogue, begin to examine their practice. Over the course of many years, I have seen it in their eyes and hear it in their language; it is a moment of surprise, often expressed as a cognitive shift (Costa & Garmston, 2002; Schon, 1987). Through a cognitive process, the person actually begins to think in different ways. The evidence of the shift in thinking is observable in a person's newly stated beliefs and intentional actions as well as in physical and emotional reactions. We can actually detect the energy to do things differently by observing facial and posture changes.

REFLECTIONS ON ENTITLEMENT: A MYSTIC ELEMENTARY SCHOOL CONVERSATION

Acknowledging and owning one's feelings or reactions is a first step in being able to productively confront issues of oppression in our schools and communities. Our two educator colleagues at Mystic School again provide illustrative conversation. Suzanne is identifying how she has acknowledged her feelings when examining the deeper issues of privilege and entitlement related to how students are performing. She is warming to the notion of how she can make constructive choices that influence the learning of students:

Clara: It sure seems to me that you have personalized this entire presentation. I sat at the same table as you, but had a very different reaction.

Suzanne: What do you mean?

Clara: I related the speaker's presentation to our current work on serving the needs of students identified as "under-performing." I must admit to moments of discomfort when she asked us to substitute "under-served" for "under-performing." Yes, I do feel a twinge when we realize schools have unacknowledged systems of oppression. But I have begun to focus on her comment, "When you feel that twinge of emotion, look to see if you are on the verge of deeper learning." For me, the deeper learning is involved with how we can become effective with students who are not being successful in our schools.

Suzanne: Well, if their parents don't even care. . . .

Clara: Wait just a minute! You are feeding into just what the presenter described.

Suzanne: What do you mean?

Clara: By focusing solely on the parents, you are not considering the power, authority, and influence we have as educators. If we believe our students have the capacity to learn, then we can learn new, different, and better ways in which to teach them. You do remember the EdTrust PowerPoint presentation, don't you? The one in which numerous schools with demographics just like ours are being very successful? It is about our taking responsibility to research, to find, and to use materials and approaches that work for our students and for us.

Suzanne is being coached by Clara to look beyond her initial, personal reaction and examine her underlying assumptions about her students and their parents. Suzanne is on the verge of being able to exercise direct influence over how she views and works with her students and their parents. At this point, Suzanne, if she so chooses, will be more able and willing to begin examining her practice—the one thing over which she has total control—to see how she can work differently with her students. As Suzanne experiences this transition, she will feel more empowered. Her empowerment is her personal transformation.

REFLECTIVE ACTIVITY

What is your reaction to this section on anger, guilt, or confidence? In what ways does this information inform your practice? How will you take this information into professional conversations with your colleagues? Please use the space below to record your thinking.

_____

_____

_____

_____

CARRYING OUR LEARNING FORWARD

Feelings of anger, guilt, and self-confidence can be our responses to new information. Similarly, new information could generate reactions that range from oppression to entitlement with and self-determination/ personal responsibility as a midpoint. Figure 5.3 represents a range of reactions in linear form, from oppression to entitlement, with self-determination and personal responsibility being the midpoint. In the same way that anger and guilt are opposite feelings and reactions, oppression and entitlement are opposite behaviors, and they too can lead to being paralyzed and dysfunctional in making effective changes for our schools. The midpoint of this continuum represents self-determination for those who are from historically oppressed groups, and it represents personal responsibility for those who are from privileged and entitled groups. The common denominator for both the oppressed and the entitled members is that they have constructive, functional choices to make and actions to take as educators.

Oppression is the consequence of racism, sexism, ethnocentrism, or heterosexism. Overt acts of oppression serve to deny the benefits of society to people based on their group membership. Throughout our history, educational practices that fostered oppression in schools included tracking programs and ability grouping. Regardless of how well intended these programs might have been at the time, they precluded or limited

Figure 5.3   Oppression–Entitlement Continuum

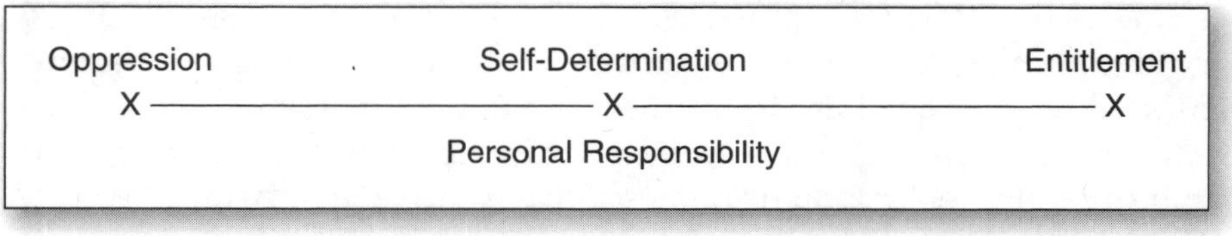

Oppression	Self-Determination	Entitlement
X —————————	X ——————————	X
	Personal Responsibility	

mobility for specific ethnic or racial groups. Ultimately, the consequences of these programs were chronic achievement gaps among demographic groups of students, disparate suspension and expulsion rates, and Eurocentric curricula that rendered women and people of color invisible. Less obvious, though no less harmful, acts of oppression include lowered expectations, biased testing, and ethnocentric history and literature textbooks. Biased testing creates a reverse affirmative action. Ethnocentric textbooks have given the dominant society a mythical view of its role in the growth of this country and made all others invisible, exotic, or dehumanized. These practices are a significant part of our history and culture that for too long state departments of education and major publishers have tried to ignore. In this twenty-first century, with the availability of top-quality multicultural materials, continuing to disregard our country's authentic history and literature might be the ultimate sense of entitlement and privilege. Several states are now considering clearly revisionist history curricula and the nightly news is replete with unsubstantiated allegations of "fake news" and "alternative facts." If educators do not have knowledge of our history and culture as it occurred as opposed to frequently used sanitized Eurocentric depictions, we will regress in ways that is a disservice to all students and educators in our schools.

Self-Determination. When issues of oppression are raised, many educators from historically oppressed groups often become agitated and angry that others are either naïve or resistant to hearing about experiences of being marginalized and oppressed. For people from historically oppressed groups, the struggle is to recognize systemic and systematic oppression and to commit oneself to self-determination. The ultimate oppression could be for a person to accept the notion that education is so hopelessly racist, sexist, ethnocentric, or heterosexist that there is little one can do. This position robs one of personal power. On the other hand, educators from historically oppressed groups who understand oppression are able to confront dysfunctional systems and to develop networks of allies to take control of their personal and professional lives. Such educators are not swayed by tokenism and work with their colleagues to lead in developing policies and practices that narrow and close achievement opportunities and outcomes.

A Personal Moral Imperative. The magnitude of the challenge for many educators who learn of privilege and entitlement for the first time rests on the extent to which they have failed to recognize, let alone acknowledge, systemic practices that now seem so apparent. Initial awareness often leads to expressions of disgust as well as denial that they have directly benefited from the systematic oppression of others. Awareness of and acknowledgement of entitlement is a sign of growth and strength. Understanding oppression and entitlement is the first step to self-determination and personal responsibility.

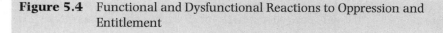

Figure 5.4   Functional and Dysfunctional Reactions to Oppression and Entitlement

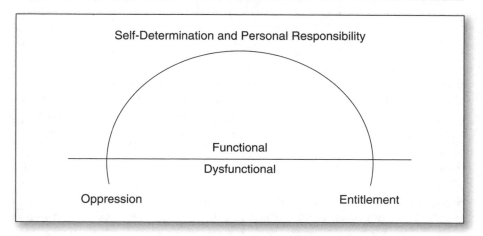

Figure 5.4 presents oppression and entitlement as being similarly dysfunctional. The functional alternatives are self-determination and personal responsibility.

Understanding and recognizing persistent systemic oppression combined with understanding and recognizing the benefits of entitlement are necessary in educators making moral decisions. To do nothing, once informed, is tantamount to the immoral position of conspirator. The moral position is to commit oneself to end the inequities fostered openly or benignly in schools. Although entitled people can work with marginalized, oppressed groups, their major responsibility is to work within schools and districts to raise the consciousness of uninformed colleagues. Morality is not arrogance. Once I discover my moral purpose, I do not become *better than* the colleagues who still struggle with who they are in relation to the communities they serve. I cannot change another person if that person is not willing to examine his own values, beliefs, and assumptions in relation to the students and families he serves. Leading from a moral position centers on changing policies, practices, and behaviors that perpetuate oppression and entitlement. Culturally Proficient educators recognize the interconnectedness of oppression and entitlement as well as the interconnectedness of values and behaviors.

Comparable to the shift from anger and guilt to confidence, educators who transcend oppression and entitlement opt for self-determination and personal responsibility. Culturally proficient educators demonstrate the ability and willingness to reflect on their practices for the purpose of providing their students access to high-quality educational experiences. Culturally Proficient educators demonstrate the ability to reflect on their practice for the purpose of continuous improvement. The shift in thinking is from cultural destructiveness, cultural incapacity, and cultural blindness to cultural precompetence and cultural competence. The language of these educators shifts from, "What's wrong with these students, their parents, their cultures . . . ?" to statements such as, "In what ways can we use this information to drive our professional learning this year?"

Confronting one's unacknowledged privileges with respect to institutional values, policies, and practices that perpetuate disparity takes the will to see what can be disquieting information and, then, takes personal commitment to moral authority. School leaders can be pivotal in ensuring that we, all of us, are part of the discussions about diversity. Let us revisit Suzanne and Clara, who have been talking about these issues, and see how they are handling these topics:

Suzanne: Okay, so I am beginning to understand. My feelings are more about resistance than anything. I can see that now. I can't say that I am totally comfortable with this whole notion yet, but I can appreciate that we have to do something. I am beginning to understand your feedback that I want to "short-circuit" the system of learning about cultural proficiency.

Clara: With that, we can make a start. How is it you recognize, within yourself, that you have been avoiding the deeper learning?

Suzanne: Well, it has to do with the presentation the other day. I have been thinking—no, hoping—that all of this fuss about diversity was that I was going to need to learn particular strategies in working with low-performing students.

Clara: How do you see it now?

Suzanne: I am not totally certain, but I know it has to involve my looking at what I expect from my students, how I interact with them, and my knowledge of how students learn. In some ways, it is as if I am starting all over again as a teacher.

Clara: Yes, it is about learning and unlearning; however, the main difference between now and when we began our roles as educators is that we have a storehouse of knowledge of what does and what does not work.

Suzanne: Well, this diversity training must be awfully burdensome for you.

Clara: How do you mean?

Suzanne: You already know all of this stuff, don't you?

Clara: Hardly! Though I am a person of color, there is much for me to learn about working with all groups. However, probably the most important role I see for myself is to make sure that I keep these issues on the table for all of us to face. That is a challenge that I welcome.

Suzanne: Yeah. And, that is a challenge I have to share with you. It is like the speaker said the other day: "We have to approach each of these students like we would want people to approach our own children." That sure makes it personal.

Being culturally precompetent entails becoming aware and knowing what you do not know. It is not having the answers but being able to know when current practices are not serving students. Culturally precompetent educators demonstrate a willingness to learn about their students' cultures, learning styles, and the communities in which they live. Culturally competent educators reflect on their practices using the lens of the five Essential Elements of Cultural Competence that appear in the next chapter—assessing their cultural knowledge, valuing diversity, managing the dynamics of difference, adapting to diversity, and institutionalizing cultural knowledge.

Culturally proficient educators are committed to the inside-out approach of cultural proficiency as they continuously examine their values and behaviors and seek to improve their individual practice and contribute to a vital learning community in their school or district.

GOING DEEPER

In what ways do you describe systemic oppression? Then, in what ways do you describe privilege and entitlement? What is your reaction to the concepts of systemic oppression, privilege, and entitlement? How has this chapter informed your learning? In what ways might responses to these questions deepen your inside-out learning? What questions do you have to guide your continued learning? Please use the space below to record your responses.

_____

_____

_____

_____

DIALOGIC ACTIVITY

In what ways will you apply your learning from this chapter to your educator role? How might the information from this chapter guide you and your colleagues in examining your grade level or department or school's policies and practices relative to inclusivity and access? What questions would guide the inquiry? Please use the space below to record your group's responses.

_____

_____

_____

_____

CHAPTER 6

Going Forward Takes Commitment and Effort: It Always Has

These five verbs are what we need to move forward!

—Superintendent, 2015

The purpose of this book is closely tied to the opportunity afforded by the current ferment stemming from the 2016 primary and general elections. Being on the right or the left of the political spectrum is, I believe, immaterial. In fact, I surmise that the same level of discord would be with us if another candidate had won the presidency and/or control of Congress.

Our political context is, to a large degree, somewhat extraneous. What we must pay attention to was referred to earlier as "the noise." That stated, possibly, the prevalence of ever-expanding forms of social media have emboldened some people to express antisocial beliefs more strongly and assertively than in any other national campaign in memory. Expressions of stress and angst abound. As educators, we are not sheltered from these expressions as they often emerge from our students, from community members, and among educators. As pointed out in Chapters 2 to 4, our country has experienced cyclical periods where systemic oppression in forms of racism, xenophobia, and other forms of bigotry spew forth. As of this writing, expressions of intolerance and bigotry have emerged in some of our schools in terms of hate speech, graffiti, and targeted social media messages. The burden this places on teachers, counselors, and administrators is immense.

My suggestion here is based on the premise of these events being cyclical. Now is the time for us to develop mechanisms and strategies to prepare ourselves and recognize that the next cycle is under way. Expressions of tribalism or nationalism abound in Europe where, like sectors of our country, multiculturalism is demonized as a failed experiment. We must lead in ways that schools and school districts learn to be inclusive in every sense of the word. Beginning now, we will prepare ourselves and our schools for the next cycle of noise as our nation evolves, and hopefully, matures over the next three, five, or twenty years. Yes, we will face walls and barriers, but we must learn to build more bridges and open more doors, even in the face of conflict. A wise colleague advised early in my career, "If you anticipate conflict on the horizon, go ahead and initiate it. In that way, you are more likely to channel all that energy into more productive outcomes."

Cross's 1989 seminal work on Cultural Competence that serves as the basis for the work of Cultural Proficiency clearly articulates the barriers of systemic oppression, a sense of privilege and entitlement, resistance to change, and unawareness of the need to adapt (see Table 4.1) as impediments to developing an inclusive society. In previous work on Cultural Proficiency, my colleagues and I positioned the Barriers into a specific tool, Overcoming Barriers to Cultural Proficiency. With the tool defined and operationalized in Chapter 5, educators are well prepared to deepen what Cross (1989) describes as personal and professional inside-out change.

The Cultural Proficiency journey is a personal and professional voyage without a distinct beginning and certainly without an end. Cultural Proficiency is a journey of becoming, a journey of continuous learning. Cultural Proficiency is not a goal attained. Cultural Proficiency is not an amount of knowledge learned. Cultural Proficiency is not the consequence of successfully completing a test (other than the test of life, that is ☺). Cultural Proficiency entails development of core values that guide educators and their schools engaged in inclusive practices that serve the academic and social needs of diverse student groups and the communities in which they live. Culturally Proficient educators are invested in their own learning and lead their schools and school districts to learn from the communities they serve. Culturally Proficient educators prepare students to live in a world of difference.

Cultural Proficiency is a two-step process—explication of core values that inform professional and institutional vision and mission statements, and professional behaviors and institutional policies and practices carefully and intentionally aligned with those espoused values. Cross offers Guiding Principles to inform core values and Essential Elements to guide professional behavior and institutional practices. Metaphorically, the Guiding Principles serve as guidepost and the Essential Elements function as worker bees.

THE BLARING OF TRUMPETS

Our country is at an important crossroads and our schools must provide prominent voices in promoting inclusivity. In our almost 250-year existence we have repeatedly contended with oppressive social forces. History exists to teach us. While this country has accomplished much in our curvy road to becoming inclusive of women, communities of color, low socioeconomic groups, and homosexual and transgender people, we are now being tested in ways that could derail progress made to date. Or, we can stand together, inclusive of all groups, as allies and advocates, and confront the voices that would have us regress.

As previously indicated, educators and schools that are intentionally inclusive engage in an adaptive process where educators examine their values and behaviors and, then, examine their policies and practices. When educators and their schools align their values, beliefs, and behaviors, they can more clearly and intentionally serve the educational needs of the cultural groups of students in their schools. Anything less runs the risk of devolving into a society of intractable "haves" and "have nots."

The Cultural Proficiency Framework guides educators in a transformative inside-out examination of individual educators' core values and schools' core values expressed as policies. Once core values are inclusive of the students served by the school, educators and their schools are prepared to examine educator behaviors and schools' prevalent practices.

The five Essential Elements of Cultural Competence serve as standards for guiding educator behaviors and schools' policies and practices. One of my favorite stories about the power of the Essential Elements is from a school district Delores and I work with. After an initial session with the Superintendents' Leadership Team where the Framework and Tools of Cultural Proficiency were introduced and discussed in depth, the Team committed to a study of *Culturally Proficient Leadership.* They met monthly and discussed the book chapter by chapter. During one of those sessions, the superintendent exclaimed, "These Five Essential Elements are exactly what we need to guide the work of our district! Everything we do fits within these five actions." The important learning is that Cultural Proficiency is a journey of continuous learning and it is a journey that provides educators with a lens through which to examine their current work. Importantly, Cultural Proficiency provides the Essential Elements as standards for framing educators' values and behaviors and schools' policies and practices.

Consideration of the Guiding Principles and Essential Elements is readily organized into an overlapping two-phase process:

PHASE 1: THE GUIDING PRINCIPLES OF CULTURAL PROFICIENCY

In his initial work Cross (1989) lists twenty-two Guiding Principles for use in social service agencies. In our first book, Raymond, Kikanza, and I (1999) culled five Guiding Principles from Cross's original list as being pertinent to education. As our facility and experience with the Tools of Cultural Proficiency matured, periodically we return to Cross's original list seeking more jewels. As of now, we use nine of Cross's Guiding Principles. In 2010 the Guiding Principles were first published as questions followed by discussion in the administrative journal *Leadership* for the Association of California School Administrators (Lindsey, 2010).

NINE KEY QUESTIONS FOR REFLECTION AND DIALOGUE

The Guiding Principles are intended to inform conversations among educators and related community members in ways that participants probe their own beliefs about the communities being served by the school or school district. It is recommended that participants use the material below to engage in dialogue for the purpose of arriving at shared understanding. Once shared understanding of the Guiding Principles is achieved, it is important for participants to examine the school or school districts' current vision, mission, and core values through the lens of their newly shared understanding.

To what extent do you honor culture as a natural and normal part of the community you serve?

California's Public Accountability Act and No Child Left Behind have brought us face to face with the reality of cultural demographic groups in ways that we have never before faced in this country. Though always present, we now have the opportunity to discuss student learning in terms of race, ethnicity, gender, ableness, and language learning. Each of us, as an educator and as a school district, must recognize the extent to which we regard these, and other cultural groupings, as asset-rich resources on which to build our educational programs, and not as accountability inconveniences, deficits, or sources of problems. Following each of the Guiding Principles is a brief discussion of the relevance of the principle to having inclusive schools.

To what extent do you recognize and understand the differential and historical treatment accorded to those least well served in our schools?

The disparities that we have come to acknowledge as the achievement or learning gap in many cases have been developed over many generations.

Though we probably have not been party to intentional practices of segregation, racism, sexism, ethnocentrism, or any other form of oppression, it is our collective responsibility to recognize the historical and current bases of discrimination and assume responsibility for rectifying and correcting past injustices through socially just actions now. Initiating socially just actions begins with recognizing how many of us today have privileges earned by being members of dominant groups. Responsibility for change must begin with those of us in the education community and the manner in which we see the achievement/learning gap as *our* issue.

When working with people whose culture is different from yours, to what extent do you see the person as both an individual and as a member of a cultural group?

We estimate that all of us like to be seen and valued for who we are. We might enjoy being part of a team that achieves; however, one's group identity does not detract from also wanting to be appreciated for who we are as a person. Yet when working in cross-cultural venues, some educators too often revert to use of terms such as "they" and "them" when referencing people from cultural groups different from themselves. At best, this often gives rise to the model minority syndrome that occurs when one member of the dominated group learns the cultural norms of the dominant group and, at worst, leads to pitting one cultural group against another and asks, "Why can't you be like _____ (the other group)?" or other forms of scapegoating.

To what extent do you recognize and value the differences within the cultural communities you serve?

The cultural groups in our schools are no more monoliths than those of us educators who populate the ranks within our schools. Each of the cultural groups we serve has vast differences in education, incomes, faith practices, and lifestyles. The cultural groups in our school communities are as diverse as is the broader community. The socioeconomic differences within cultural groups often gives rise to groups having more similar worldviews across socioeconomic lines that they do within cultural groups.

To what extent do you know and respect the unique needs of cultural groups in the community you serve?

A one-size-fits-all approach to education can serve the needs of school at the expense of the needs of our students and their communities. Even schools that have all students conform to grooming standards and physical accommodations have learned to acknowledge in their curriculum and in their teaching different learning styles, different cognitive styles, and the different ways people process information. The inclusive educator teaches and encourages colleagues to make the necessary adaptations in how schools provide educational service so that all people have access to the same benefits and privileges as members of the dominant group in society.

To what extent do you know how cultural groups in your community define family and the manner in which family serves as the primary system of support for students?

Prevalent educational practice has been to assume that parents and other family caregivers who really care about the education of their children will avail themselves of opportunities to interact with the school. Increasingly, our schools have become adept at finding culturally inclusive ways of engaging parents and caregivers in support of student achievement.

We find, too often, educators and parents have different perceptions of the term "parent participation." Lawson used the terms "communitycentric" and "schoolcentric" to describe these contrasting perceptions.

- *Communitycentric.* "Parents involved in activities that meet the basic needs of their children as going to school well fed, rested, and clean."
- *Schoolcentric.* "Parents involved in activities that are structured and defined for parents by schools." (Lawson as cited in Lindsey et al., 2009, p. 105)

Effective and meaningful partnerships between parents and schools require sensitive, respectful, and caring school leaders willing to learn the positive nature and culture of the community as well as to identify barriers that have impeded progress in school–community relations. Tahoe Elementary School in Sacramento, California, and San Marcos Elementary School in San Marcos, California, have identified their core values about parent/guardian involvement and have been successful in engaging parents in productive ways through school-site, home, and other off-site meetings.

The traditional, often stereotypic, image of Euro-American homes of family identified as one mother, one father, and the children is now recognized as a limited view of family. Today, culturally proficient school leaders acknowledge single-parent families, multiple-generation extended families, same-gender parents, foster care homes, and residential care homes as family. Whatever the configuration for the children in our schools, their family is their family.

To what extent do you recognize and understand the bicultural reality for cultural groups historically not well served in our schools?

Parents/guardians and their children have to be fluent in the communication patterns of the school as well as the communication patterns that exist in their communities. They also have to know the cultural norms and expectations of schools, which might conflict or be different from those in their communities, their countries of origin or their cultural groups. In ideal conditions, their children are developing bicultural skills, learning to code switch to meet the cultural expectations of their environments. However, parents might not have these skills for adapting to new and different environments. Parents/guardians and their children are then penalized because they do not respond to the norms set by educators when they do not navigate well the educational systems of the public schools.

To what extent do you recognize your role in acknowledging, adjusting to, and accepting cross-cultural interactions as necessary social and communications dynamics?

We have encountered few educators who fail to recognize the historical and current impact of racism and other forms of oppression on current school environments. It is also our experience that our educator colleagues who do recognize and understand the huge toll that oppression takes also understand how people not affected by those same systems benefit in unwitting ways. It is precisely the awareness of the dynamic nature of oppression vs. entitlement that enables such educators to be effective in responding to the educational needs of cultural groups within their schools/districts.

Unless one has experienced intentional or unintentional acts of discrimination or oppression, one cannot fathom the everyday toll it takes on day-to-day life experiences. The overrepresentation of students of color in special education programs and their underrepresentation in advanced placement and gifted and talented programs is not new. Educators who are aware of such dynamics employ strategies and tactics that engage parents as partners in beneficial placements for their children.

To what extent do you incorporate cultural knowledge into educational practices and policy-making?

Experienced educational leaders recognize the need to learn the culture of a new organization. Their very survival depends on appropriate responses to cultural norms of the school community. Effective educational leaders, additionally, are aware of their own cultures and the impact their culture has on their school/district. Knowledge about school culture, our individual cultures, and the cultures of our community rarely arrives to our desktops in a three-ring notebook or a PDF file. Cultural knowledge is possessed by those who are keenly aware of themselves, their community surroundings, and the legacies and challenges experienced by cultural groups in our country and local communities.

Educational leaders who possess this self-awareness and are effective in cross-cultural settings avoid phrases such as, "Doesn't everyone know that . . . ?," or "I would hope parents see that as their responsibility," or "It's the way we do things here and they will have to adjust." Phrases such as these marginalize outsiders and serve to perpetuate an "us against them" mentality.

Culturally proficient leaders share their own cultural knowledge, engage with the community, and invite community experts knowing that such actions, over time, will lead to appropriately institutionalizing cultural knowledge. Such leaders recognize that reculturing schools to be responsive to diverse constituencies is an internal and intentional process.

Responses to these nine questions can be the basis for core values, vision statements, and vision statements that inform and support for culturally proficient leadership. The principles help frame and focus the behaviors of teachers and school leaders intentionally on all students learning at levels higher than ever before.

USE INTERNAL ASSETS AND BE INTENTIONAL

Learning gaps are ours to rectify. Shifting the culture of a school district from responding to learning gaps as compliance issues to responding in ways that transform organizational culture relies on use of school leaders' internal assets of reflection and dialogue. This intentionality and mindfulness is a two-step process of personal reflection and purposeful dialogue with colleagues. Dialogic discussions about these nine questions provide the basis for developing vision and mission statements and core values intended to serve a diverse community. To be effective in schools today leaders need strong core personal and organizational values (Collins & Porras, 1997; Lindsey, 2009; Senge, 2000). In addition to the values you currently hold, the values of cultural proficiency explicit in the nine Guiding Principles can serve as the foundation on which to reculture and transform schools/districts (Lindsey, Nuri Robins, Terrell, & Lindsey, 2010).

PHASE 2: THE ESSENTIAL ELEMENTS OF CULTURAL COMPETENCE

Extending the earlier metaphor in which the Tools, Overcoming Barriers and Guiding Principles, function as twin pillars in the foundation of the Cultural Proficiency Framework (Table 4.1), the five Essential Elements can be interconnected rooms atop the foundation. Each room has a distinct function in this metaphor where a house becomes a home when it is carefully nurtured. As inclusive core values are manifest in educators' behaviors and schools' practices, students from diverse backgrounds are poised to be socially and academically successful.

Culturally proficient educators understand that effective leadership in a diverse environment is about changing the manner in which we work with those who are culturally different from ourselves. Personal transformation that facilitates institutional change inclusive of all students is the goal of Cultural Proficiency.

Leading effectively in a diverse environment is *not* about changing others: it is about our own personal work. To guide the personal work in which school leaders examine their own values and behaviors and, in due time, the policies and practices of the school, the five Essential Elements of Cultural Competence serve as standards for culturally competent and proficient educator behavior and schools and school districts' institutional practices. The Essential Elements of Cultural Competence and proficient education and leadership are

- Assessing cultural knowledge,
- Valuing diversity,
- Managing the dynamics of difference,
- Adapting to diversity, and
- Institutionalizing cultural knowledge (Lindsey, 2009).

Table 6.1 presents the Culturally Proficient Professional Learning Rubric as a useful tool for learning and planning. The rubric has several useful features:

- The rubric demonstrates the interconnectedness of the Tools of Cultural Proficiency:
  - Overcoming Barriers of systemic oppression, entitlement, resistance to change, and awareness of our need to adapt can become default core values that assume a deficit approach to students and their cultures and communities.
  - The Guiding Principles inform core values that embrace students' culture as assets on which educational experiences are constructed.
  - The Cultural Proficiency Continuum represents unhealthy and healthy educator and educational practices. The Barriers inform the unhealthy practices. In marked contrast, healthy practices are informed by the Guiding Principles and demonstrate meeting standards in the Cultural Competence column. Healthy practices in the Cultural Proficiency column demonstrate a commitment to continuous learning and improvement.
  - The Essential Elements serve as standards for educator behavior and school policies and practices.

Table 6.1 Rubric for Cultural Proficiency Professional Learning

Outcome: Increase the achievement and well-being of all students, with an emphasis on addressing achievement and opportunity disparities between student groups, by continuously improving the knowledge, skills, and attitudes of educators who educate and support them.

Five Essential Elements serve as standards for Culturally Proficient Leadership	Informed by Barriers to Cultural Proficiency — Tolerance for Diversity: Focus on "them"			Informed by Guiding Principles of Cultural Proficiency — Transformation for Equity; Focus on "our practice"		
	Cultural Destructiveness	Cultural Incapacity	Cultural Blindness	Cultural Precompetence	Cultural Competence: Standard is met	Cultural Proficiency
Assessing Cultural Knowledge identifies the differences among people in your environment; makes us aware of the importance of cultural identity; and identifies organizational culture.	**Professional learning** reinforces cultural misinformation that "we are all the same" by training educators in a single/one-size-fits-all approach to instruction and student learning.	**Professional learning** uses information about student differences as the rationale for training teachers to "get all students on board" in reaching a target considered the norm.	**Professional learning** focuses on generalized best practices for standards-based instruction that apply to all educators and students, without differentiation.	**Culturally Proficient Professional Learning** begins to reference disaggregated student and educator data about culture and adopted standards capacity in order to identify strengths and improvement areas and to determine individual and collective learning priorities.	**And . . .** actively engages educators in learning about their own cultures and examining their personal attitudes and biases in relation to staff, student, and school cultures to determine how their own assets and needs might support or hinder student success in being college and career ready.	**And . . .** integrates opportunities in real tasks to practice increased cultural knowledge about using relevant, disaggregated student and educator data to inform differentiated, culturally relevant instruction that supports students in being college and career ready.

Valuing Diversity embraces differences as contributors to the value of your environment; and addresses cultural experiences and opportunities.	Professional learning is based on developing educators' skills in removing or punishing diverse student culture, language, etc... in order to help students become successful.	Professional learning focuses on developing educators' skills to standardize student language, learning approaches, etc. to meet expectations of the dominant culture.	Professional learning reinforces strategies that lead educators not to play favorites, resulting in them ignoring cultural, linguistic, and diversity and providing all educators and/or students with the same instruction and support.	Culturally Proficient Professional Learning recognizes that educator diversity can extend professional knowledge and understanding of staff and student cultures and experiences that can help students make connections to learning and a variety of pathways to academic success.	And . . . encourages educators to work collaboratively to learn new instructional and cultural competency skills to increase the variety of approaches effective for students with a range of assets and needs to learn and thrive.	And . . . relies on educators' diverse cultures, experiences, and capabilities to develop and lead staff learning and application of differentiated instructional and support strategies required for each student to meet expectations of adopted standards.
Managing the Dynamics of Difference reframes differences so diversity is not perceived as a problem to be solved; promote, models using inquiry, dialogue related to multiple perspectives, issues arising from diversity.	Professional learning does not acknowledge diversity issues but helps educators learn how to solve people problems and quickly activate a uniform response to keep the lid on a challenging situation.	Professional learning poses diversity as a challenge that can be addressed with a foolproof solution that is tried and true.	Professional learning poses problems of practice that minimize the importance of multiple perspectives and highlights reaching consensus for the common good in order to avoid discussions about diversity that might be uncomfortable.	Culturally Proficient Professional Learning identifies and/or structures opportunities for educators to learn and practice inquiry and dialogue models that help them confidently address issues arising from multiple perspectives.	And . . . leads to the development of communities of practice where educators use inquiry and dialogue models to reframe anticipated or current issues they are facing in implementing equitable practices to address adopted expectations.	And . . . enables educators to find ways to provide students with a range of instructional approaches and supports that fit their diverse set of assets and needs and meet each different student, family, and institutional expectations that every student graduates from high school college and career ready.

Adapting to Diversity teaches and learns about differences and how to respond to them effectively, and facilitates change to meet the needs of the community.	**Professional learning** is not differentiated or purposefully connected to educator, student, or community needs.	**Professional learning** emphasizes how educators can maintain the status quo to sustain stability that students can count on.	**Professional learning** is organized as a common opportunity for all educators and consists mainly of approved programs provided by regional, state, or federal providers.	**Culturally Proficient Professional Learning** helps educators develop understanding about instructional changes required by the new Common Core standards, determine current capacities and needs to implement equity-focused policies and practices, and initiate ongoing educator learning and support to develop expertise and confidence.	**And . . .** extends educator experiences related to a variety of equity perspectives, including race, gender, language, sexual orientation, religion, special abilities and needs, and socioeconomic status that can impact students' initial ability to meet adopted expectations.	**And . . .** promotes collective action to develop and apply policies and practices that support the wide variety of instruction and support services required by diverse students engaged in meeting adopted standards and moving toward college and career.
Institutionalizing Cultural Knowledge changes systems to ensure healthy and effective responses to diversity, and shape policies and practices that meet the needs of a diverse community.	**Professional learning** does not reflect student or educator diversity or address how differentiated support is necessary to implement practices that lead to adopted standards implementation.	**Professional learning** supports approaches that reinforce values and policies ensuring that assimilation is applied in classrooms and schools.	**Professional learning** opportunities are mandated, reflecting the belief that common approaches can serve the needs of all cultural groups.	**Culturally Proficient Professional Learning** provides the means for educators to learn about and practice theories and principles of equity that can support or hinder culturally responsive policies and actions related to student learning success.	**And . . .** promotes educators developing the structure and processes for an ongoing, comprehensive system of individual and collective learning that responds to diverse and changing educator and student needs with reliable supports to meet adopted expectations that every student graduates ready to be successful in college and career.	**And . . .** includes educators' reviewing individual and collective professional learning experiences and results over time to evaluate whether professional learning efforts and changes in policies and practices are having an impact on educator effectiveness and, ultimately, all students' performance and well-being.

- The rubric serves as a teaching/learning tool to deepen understanding of the function of
  - The points along the Continuum as behavioral markers,
  - Overcoming the barriers as informing unhealthy behaviors and practices, and
  - Guiding Principles as informing healthy behaviors and practices.
- As a diagnostic instrument to gauge where you might be along the continuum, and then
- As a tool for planning action steps.

Tips for decoding the rubric

Table 6.1, Rubric for Cultural Proficiency Professional Learning reads from left to right.

- The first column presents the operational definition of each five Essential Elements in terms of professional learning.
- The sixth column, Cultural Competence, is where the standard is "met."
- The columns Cultural Precompetence to Cultural Competence to Cultural Proficiency can be considered to be developmental.
- The columns Cultural Destructiveness, Cultural Incapacity, and Cultural Blindness are not developmental (e.g., a person who is culturally destructive should not aspire to be culturally blind).

GOING DEEPER

In what ways are the Guiding Principles consistent with your beliefs about the students in your school or district? In what ways do the Guiding Principles cause you to think differently about your students? In what ways can you use the Essential Elements to guide your educational practice? What questions are surfacing for you? Please use the space below to record your thinking.

_____

_____

_____

_____

DIALOGIC ACTIVITY

Form an inquiry group and use the rubric in Table 6.1 to guide an exploration of how the group views the school. You might have individuals plot where they see the grade level, department, school, and/or district for each of the five Essential Elements. Meet and share the data. In what ways might the data inform an examination of the school's (or district's) vision, mission, and core values? In what ways might the data inform the school's (or district's) professional development and learning? Please use the space below to record your initial responses. Your responses could inform an inquiry that guides transformative change.

_____

_____

_____

_____

CHAPTER 7

My Final Thoughts and, Then, Your Turn

You have read. Most likely you have written responses to many of the reflection opportunities. If you are member of a book study group, you might have engaged in chapter-by-chapter dialogue. So, what is next?

For me, the next step is to continue to advocate for Culturally Proficient educational practices that result in students from across the demographic spectrum having equitable educational access and outcomes. I will continue to work with schools and to write as my learning about Cultural Proficiency deepens.

I am leaving this manifesto as a guide for your personal and educator journeys. Take a few moments and pen (or keyboard) responses to these questions:

- What do you see as the purpose of this book?
- To what extent was the purpose of this book successful for you? What might be evidence of that success?

_____

_____

_____

_____

_____

_____

The balance of this chapter is designed to have you expand on your responses to the two questions above and to develop a plan for you and your school or school district that enables a cultural proficiency journey for you and your colleagues in service of all students in ways that build on student and community assets.

In Chapter 6, I describe Cultural Proficiency as a two-phase process—explication of core values that inform professional and institutional vision and mission statements, and professional behaviors and institutional policies and practices carefully and intentionally aligned with those espoused values.

TWO-PHASE PROCESS—GUIDING PRINCIPLES AND ESSENTIAL ELEMENTS

This journey begins by, first, reflecting on the Guiding Principles of Cultural Proficiency in ways that will support your learning about the assumptions, values, and beliefs you hold in serving the diverse needs of your school community. Table 7.1 summarizes the Guiding Principles from Chapter 6 and presents them in question form to guide your thinking. The second step is to engage colleagues in deep dialogue about your collective responses to the questions in ways intended to arrive at shared understanding. In doing so, school vision, mission and core values become operational in the everyday life of your school and district.

Table 7.1   The Guiding Principles of Cultural Proficiency Presented as Questions to Guide Reflection and Dialogue

- To what extent do you honor culture as a natural and normal part of the community you serve?
- To what extent do you recognize and understand the differential and historical treatment accorded to those least well served in our schools?
- When working with people whose culture is different from yours, to what extent do you see the person as both an individual and as a member of a cultural group?
- To what extent do you recognize and value the differences within the cultural communities you serve?
- To what extent do you know and respect the unique needs of cultural groups in the community you serve?
- To what extent do you know how cultural groups in your community define family and the manner in which family serves as the primary system of support for students?
- To what extent do you recognize and understand the bicultural reality for cultural groups historically not well served in our schools?
- To what extent do you recognize your role in acknowledging, adjusting to, and accepting cross-cultural interactions as necessary social and communications dynamics?
- To what extent do you incorporate cultural knowledge into educational practices and policy-making?

REFLECTION

- In what ways are the Guiding Principles of Cultural Proficiency meaningful to you? How are the Guiding Principles important for your school or school district?

_____

_____

_____

_____

The Essential Elements are the action phase of this journey. Words of caution as you proceed! It is understandable that some people are anxious to get to the planning and I urge you to not give short shrift to deep consideration of the Guiding Principles before proceeding to thinking and talking about the Essential Elements. Shared understanding that arises from deep dialogue about the Guiding Principles provides consideration of students' cultures as assets on which planning is undertaken. Table 7.2 presents the Essential Elements of Cultural Competence for your use.

Table 7.2   The Essential Elements for Culturally Proficient Practices[1]

- **Assessing Cultural Knowledge:** Becoming aware of and knowing the diverse communities within your school; knowing how educators and the school as a whole reacts to marginalized communities and learn how to be effective in serving these communities. Leading and learning about the school and its grade levels and departments as cultural entities in responding to the educational needs of the underserved communities.
- **Valuing Diversity:** Creating informal and formal decision-making groups inclusive of parents/guardians and community members whose viewpoints and experiences are different from yours and the dominant group at the school, and that will enrich conversations, decision-making, and problem solving.
- **Managing the Dynamics of Difference:** Modeling problem solving and conflict resolution strategies as a natural and normal process within the culture of the schools and the diverse contexts of the communities of your school.
- **Adapting to Diversity:** Learning about underserved cultural groups different from your own; acquiring the ability to use others' experiences and backgrounds in all school settings.
- **Institutionalizing Cultural Knowledge:** Making learning about underserved cultural groups and their experiences and perspectives an integral part of the school's professional development.

1. Adapted from Delores B. Lindsey, Karen M. Kearney, Raymond D. Terrell, & Randall B. Lindsey. *A Culturally Proficient Response to the Common Core.* (2015). Thousand Oaks, CA.: Corwin Press.

- How might you use the Essential Elements to inform and guide your and your school's planning?
- Enter the date exactly one year from today: _____.
  List three commitments to guide your Cultural Proficiency journey. What might be evidence or indicators of your commitments? Please use Table 7.3 to guide your thinking.

Table 7.3   Cultural Proficiency Goals and Commitments

Date:	
Commitments/Goals	*Evidence/Indicators*
1.	
2.	
3.	

CLOSING COMMENTS

Thank you for your commitment to our children and youth. I believe that the noise will never fully abate. Additionally, I believe that our profession of education will be sorely tested in the years ahead. It is important that we not get distracted from our commitment to educate all students to their potential. I am pleased to be with you on this journey as our country continues to evolve in becoming the inclusive democracy that it can be.

I enjoy keeping in touch with colleagues such as you. My contact points are

Twitter—RBLindsey41

Web Page—under construction

Email—randallblindsey@gmail.com

References

Beatty, Barbara. (2012). Rethinking compensatory education: Historical perspectives on race, class, culture, language, and the discourse of the "disadvantaged child." *Teachers College Record, 114*(6), 1–11.

Boese, Paul. (1967, February 19). Forgiveness, quote. *The Weekly Digest, 53*(8), 146.

Borrero, Noah E., Yeh, Christine J., Crivir, I. Crux, & Suda, Jolene F. (2012). Schools as context for "othering" youth and promoting cultural assets. *Teachers College Record, 114*(2), 1–37.

Brown v. Board of Education of Topeka 347 U.S. 483 (1954).

California Department of Education. (2013, December). *The superintendent's quality professional learning standards.* Sacramento: California Department of Education, Professional Learning Support Division.

Collins, James, & Porras, Jerry. (1997). *Built to last: Successful habits of visionary companies.* New York, NY: Harper.

Costa, Art L., & Garmston, Robert J. (2002). *Cognitive coaching: A foundation for renaissance schools* (2nd ed.). Norwood, MA: Christopher-Gordon.

Cross, Terry L. (1989). *Toward a culturally competent system of care.* Washington, DC: Georgetown University Child Development Program, Child and Adolescent Service System Program.

Deal, Terrence, & Kennedy, Allan. (1982). *Corporate cultures: Understanding rites and rituals in corporate culture.* Harmondsworth, UK: Penguin.

Dilts, Robert. (1990). *Changing belief systems with NLP.* Capitola, CA: Meta.

Dilts, Robert. (1994). *Effective presentation skills.* Capitola, CA: Meta.

Freire, Paulo. (1970). *Pedagogy of the oppressed* (Nyra Bergman Ramos, trans.). New York, NY: Seabury.

Freire, Paulo. (1999). *Pedagogy of hope: Reliving pedagogy of the oppressed.* New York, NY: Continuum.

Fullan, Michael. (2003). *The moral imperative of educational leadership.* Thousand Oaks, CA: Corwin.

Gjaja, Marin, Puckett J., & Ryder, Matt. (2014). When it comes to school funding, equity is the key. *Education Week,* February 19, 30–31.

Gladwell, Michael. (2000). *The tipping point: How little things can make a big difference.* Boston, MA: Little, Brown.

Heifetz, Ron. (1994). *Leadership without easy answers.* Cambridge, MA: Belknap.

Hilliard, Asa. (1991). Do we have the will to educate all children? *Educational Leadership, 40*(1), 31–36.

Kushner, Tony. (2013). *Angels in America: A gay fantasia on national themes.* New York, NY: Theatre Communications Group.

Lau v. Nichols. (1974). 414 U.S. 563. Justia Law.

Lindsey, Delores B., Kearney, K., Estrada, D. & Lindsey, Randall B. (2015). *A culturally proficient response to the common core: Ensuring equity through professional learning.* Thousand Oaks, CA: Corwin.

Lindsey, Delores B., Lindsey, Randall B., Hord, Shirley M., & Von Frank, Valerie (2016). *Reach the highest standards in professional learning: Outcomes.* Thousand Oaks, CA: Corwin.

Lindsey, Delores B., Terrell, Raymond D., Nuri, Kikanza J. & Lindsey, Randall B. (2010, May/June). Focus on assets, overcome barriers, *Leadership,* Sacramento, CA: Association of California School Administrators, 39(5), 12–15.

Lindsey, Randall B., Karns, Michelle S., & Myatt, Keith (2010). *Culturally proficient education: An asset-based approach to conditions of poverty.* Thousand Oaks, CA: Corwin.

Lindsey, Randall B., Nuri Robins, Kikanza, & Terrell, Raymond. (1999). *Cultural proficiency: A manual for school leaders* (1st ed.). Thousand Oaks, CA.: Corwin.

Lindsey, Randall B., Nuri Robins, Kikanza, & Terrell, R. (2009). *Cultural proficiency: A manual for school leaders* (3rd ed.). Thousand Oaks, CA: Corwin.

Lindsey, Randall B., Nuri Robins, Kikanza, & Terrell, Raymond D. *Cultural Proficiency: A Manual for School Leaders (3rd Edition),* Thousand Oaks, CA: Corwin Press, 2009.

Lindsey, Randall B., Roberts, Laraine M., & CampbellJones, Franklin (2013). *The culturally proficient school: An implementation guide for school leaders* (2nd ed.). Thousand Oaks, CA: Corwin.

Loewen, James W. (1995). *Lies my teacher told me: Everything your American history textbook got wrong.* New York, NY: New Press.

Miller, Neil. (2006). *Out of the past: Gay and lesbian history from 1869 to the present.* New York, NY: Alyson Books.

Perie, Marianne, Moran, Rebecca, & Lutkus, Anthony D. (2005). *NAEP 2004 trends in academic progress: Three decades of student performance in reading and mathematics* (NCES 2005-464). Washington, DC: U.S. Department of Education, Institute of Education Sciences, National Center for Education Statistics.

Polis, Jared, & Gibson, Chris. (2014). Broadband access is critical. *Education Week,* February 19, p. 30.

The Regional Equity Assistance Centers. (2013). *How the Common Core must ensure equity by fully preparing every student for postsecondary success: Recommendations from the Regional Equity Assistance Centers on implementation of the Common Core State Standards.* San Francisco, CA: WestEd.

Schein, Edgar H. (1992). *Organizational culture and leadership.* San Francisco, CA: Jossey-Bass.

Schein, Edgar H. (2010). *Organizational culture and leadership* (4th ed.). San Francisco, CA: Jossey-Bass.

Schon, Donald A. (1987). *Educating the reflective practitioner: Toward a new design for teaching and learning in the professions.* San Francisco, CA: Jossey-Bass.

Senge, Peter M., Cambron-McCabe, Nelda, Lucas, Timothy, Kleiner, Art, Dutton, James, & Smith, Bryan (Eds.). (2000). *Schools that learn: A fifth discipline fieldbook for educators, parents, and everyone who cares about education.* New York: Doubleday.

Shields, Carolyn. (2010). Transformative leadership: Working for equity in diverse contexts. *Educational Administration Quarterly, 46,* 558–589.

Span, Christopher, & Rivers, Ishwanzya D. (2012). Reassessing the achievement gap: An intergenerational comparison of African American student achievement before and after compensatory education and the Elementary and Secondary Education Act. *Teachers College Record, 114*(6), 1–17. Retrieved from http://www.tcrecord.org; ID Number: 16690.

Spencer, John. (2013). *Equality in education law and policy, 1954–2010.* Cambridge, MA: Cambridge University Press.

Superfine, Benjamin Michael. (2013). *Equality in education law and policy, 1954–2010.* Cambridge, MA: Cambridge University Press.

Wagner, Tony, Kegan, Robert, Lahey, Lisa, Lemons, Richard W., Garnier, Jude, Helsing, Deborah, . . . , & Rasmussen, Harriette Thurber. (2006). *Change leadership: A practical guide to transforming our schools.* San Francisco, CA: Jossey-Bass WestEd.

Weick, Karl. (1979). *The social psychology of organizing* (2nd ed.). New York, NY: McGraw-Hill.

Resources

CULTURAL PROFICIENCY BOOKS' ESSENTIAL QUESTIONS

Corwin Cultural Proficiency Books	Authors	Focus and Essential Questions
Cultural Proficiency: A Manual for School Leaders, 3rd ed., 2009	Randall B. Lindsey Kikanza Nuri Robins Raymond D. Terrell	This book is an introduction to Cultural Proficiency. The book provides readers with extended discussion of each of the tools and the historical framework for diversity work. • What is Cultural Proficiency? How does Cultural Proficiency differ from other responses to diversity? • In what ways do I incorporate the Tools of Cultural Proficiency into my practice? • How do I use the resources and activities to support professional learning? • How do I identify barriers to student learning? • How do the Guiding Principles and Essential Elements support better education for students? • What does the inside-out process mean for me as an educator? • How do I foster challenging conversations with colleagues? • How do I extend my own learning?

(Continued)

(Continued)

Corwin Cultural Proficiency Books	Authors	Focus and Essential Questions
Culturally Proficient Instruction: A Guide for People Who Teach, **3rd ed., 2012**	Kikanza Nuri-Robins Randall B. Lindsey Delores B. Lindsey Raymond D. Terrell	This book focuses on the five Essential Elements and can be helpful to anyone in an instructional role. This book can be used as a workbook for a study group. • What does it mean to be a culturally proficient instructor? • How do I incorporate Cultural Proficiency into a school's learning community processes? • How do we move from mindset or mental model to a set of practices in our school? • How does my cultural story support being effective as an educator with my students? • In what ways might we apply the Maple View Story to our learning community? • In what ways can I integrate the Guiding Principles of Cultural Proficiency with my own values about learning and learners? • In what ways do the Essential Elements as standards inform and support our work with the Common Core standards? • How do I foster challenging conversations with colleagues? • How do I extend my own learning?
The Culturally Proficient School: An Implementation Guide for School Leaders, **2nd ed., 2013**	Randall B. Lindsey Laraine M. Roberts Franklin CampbellJones	This book guides the reader to examine her school as a cultural organization and to design and implement approaches to dialogue and inquiry. • In what ways do Cultural Proficiency and school leadership help me close achievement gaps? • What are the communication skills I need to master to support my colleagues when focusing on achievement gap topics? • How do transactional and transformational changes differ and inform closing achievement gaps in my school/district? • How do I foster challenging conversations with colleagues? • How do I extend my own learning?

Corwin Cultural Proficiency Books	Authors	Focus and Essential Questions
Culturally Proficient Coaching: Supporting Educators to Create Equitable Schools, 2007	Delores B. Lindsey Richard S. Martinez Randall B. Lindsey	This book aligns the Essential Elements with Costa and Garmston's Cognitive Coaching model. The book provides coaches, teachers, and administrators a personal guidebook with protocols and maps for conducting conversations that shift thinking in support of all students achieving at levels higher than ever before. • What are the coaching skills I need in working with diverse student populations? • In what ways do the Tools of Cultural Proficiency and Cognitive Coaching's States of Mind support my addressing achievement issues in my school? • How do I foster challenging conversations with colleagues? • How do I extend my own learning?
Culturally Proficient Inquiry: A Lens for Identifying and Examining Educational Gaps, 2008	Randall B. Lindsey Stephanie M. Graham R. Chris Westphal, Jr. Cynthia L. Jew	This book uses protocols for gathering and analyzing student achievement and access data. Rubrics for gathering and analyzing data about educator practices are also presented. A CD accompanies the book for easy downloading and use of the data protocols. • How do we move from the will to educate all children to actually developing our skills and doing so? • In what ways do we use the various forms of student achievement data to inform educator practice? • In what ways do we use access data (e.g., suspensions, absences, enrollment in special education or gifted classes) to inform schoolwide practices? • How do we use the four rubrics to inform educator professional learning? • How do I foster challenging conversations with colleagues? • How do I extend my own learning?

(Continued)

(Continued)

Corwin Cultural Proficiency Books	Authors	Focus and Essential Questions
Culturally Proficient Leadership: The Personal Journey Begins Within, 2009	Raymond D. Terrell Randall B. Lindsey	This book guides the reader through the development of a cultural autobiography as a means to becoming an increasingly effective leader in our diverse society. The book is an effective tool for use by leadership teams. • How did I develop my attitudes about others' cultures? • When I engage in intentional cross-cultural communication, how can I use those experiences to heighten my effectiveness? • In what ways can I grow into being a culturally proficient leader? • How do I foster challenging conversations with colleagues? • How do I extend my own learning?
Culturally Proficient Learning Communities: Confronting Inequity Through Collaborative Curiosity, 2009	Delores B. Lindsey Linda D. Jungwirth Jarvis V.N.C. Pahl Randall B. Lindsey	This book provides readers a lens through which to examine the purpose, the intentions, and the progress of learning communities to which they belong or wish to develop. School and district leaders are provided protocols, activities, and rubrics to engage in actions focused on the intersection of race, ethnicity, gender, social-class, sexual orientation and identity, faith, and ableness with the disparities in student achievement. • What is necessary for a learning community to become a "culturally proficient learning community?" • What is organizational culture and how do I describe my school's culture in support of equity and access? • What are "curiosity" and "collaborative curiosity," and how do I foster them at my school/district? • How will "breakthrough questions" enhance my work as a learning community member and leader? • How do I foster challenging conversations with colleagues? • How do I extend my own learning?

Corwin Cultural Proficiency Books	Authors	Focus and Essential Questions
***The Cultural Proficiency Journey: Moving Beyond Ethical Barriers Toward Profound School Change**, 2010*	Franklin CampbellJones Brenda CampbellJones Randall B. Lindsey	This book explores Cultural Proficiency as an ethical construct. It makes transparent the connection between values, assumptions, and beliefs, and observable behavior, making change possible and sustainable. The book is appropriate for book study teams. • In what ways does "moral consciousness" inform and support my role as an educator? • How does a school's "core values" become reflected in assumptions held about students? • What steps do I take to ensure that my school and I understand any low expectations we might have? • How do we recognize that our low expectations serve as ethical barriers? • How do I foster challenging conversations with colleagues? • How do I extend my own learning?
***Culturally Proficient Education: An Asset-Based Response to Conditions of Poverty**, 2010*	Randall B. Lindsey Michelle S. Karns Keith Myatt	This book is written for educators to learn how to identify and develop the strengths of students from low-income backgrounds. It is an effective learning community resource to promote reflection and dialogue. • What are "assets" that students bring to school? • How do we operate from an "assets-based" perspective? • What are my and my school's expectations about students from low-income and impoverished backgrounds? • How do I foster challenging conversations with colleagues? • How do I extend my own learning?

(Continued)

(Continued)

Corwin Cultural Proficiency Books	Authors	Focus and Essential Questions
Culturally Proficient Collaboration: Use and Misuse of School Counselors, 2011	Diana L. Stephens Randall B. Lindsey	This book uses the lens of Cultural Proficiency to frame the American Association of School Counselors' performance standards and the Education Trust's Transforming School Counseling Initiative as means for addressing issues of access and equity in schools in collaborative school leadership teams. • How do counselors fit into achievement-related conversations with administrators and teachers? • What is the "new role" for counselors? • How does this "new role" differ from existing views of school counselor? • What is the role of site administrators in this new role of school counselor? • How do I foster challenging conversations with colleagues? • How do I extend my own learning?
A Culturally Proficient Society Begins in School: Leadership for Equity, 2011	Carmella S. Franco Maria G. Ott Darline P. Robles	This book frames the life stories of three superintendents through the lens of Cultural Proficiency. The reader is provided the opportunity to design or modify his or her own leadership for equity plan. • In what ways is the role of school superintendent related to equity issues? • Why is this topic important to me as a superintendent or aspiring superintendent? • What are the leadership characteristics of a Culturally Proficient school superintendent? • How do I foster challenging conversations with colleagues? • How do I extend my own learning?

Corwin Cultural Proficiency Books	Authors	Focus and Essential Questions
The Best of Corwin: Equity, 2012	Randall B. Lindsey, Ed.	This edited book provides a range of perspectives of published chapters from prominent authors on topics of equity, access, and diversity. It is designed for use by school study groups. <ul><li>In what ways do these readings support our professional learning?</li><li>How might I use these readings to engage others in learning conversations to support all students learning and all educators educating all students?</li></ul>
Culturally Proficient Practice: Supporting Educators of English Learning Students, 2012	Reyes L. Quezada Delores B. Lindsey Randall B. Lindsey	This book guides readers to apply the 5 Essential Elements of Cultural Competence to their individual practice and their school's approaches to equity. The book works well for school study groups. <ul><li>In what ways do I foster support for the education of English learning students?</li><li>How can I use action research strategies to inform my practice with English learning students?</li><li>In what ways might this book support all educators in our district/school?</li><li>How do I foster challenging conversations with colleagues?</li><li>How do I extend my own learning?</li></ul>

(Continued)

(Continued)

Corwin Cultural Proficiency Books	Authors	Focus and Essential Questions
A Culturally Proficient Response to LGBT Communities: A Guide for Educators, 2013	Randall B. Lindsey Richard Diaz Kikanza Nuri-Robins Raymond D. Terrell Delores B. Lindsey	This book guides the reader to understand sexual orientation in a way that provides for the educational needs of all students. The reader explores values, behaviors, policies, and practices that impact lesbian, gay, bisexual and transgender (LGBT) students, educators, and parents/guardians. • How do I foster support for LGBT colleagues, students, and parents/guardians? • In what ways does our school represent a value for LGBT members? • How can I create a safe environment for all students to learn? • To what extent is my school an environment where it is safe for the adults to be open about their sexual orientation? • How do I reconcile my attitudes toward religion and sexuality with my responsibilities as a PreK–12 educator? • How do I foster challenging conversations with colleagues? • How do I extend my own learning?
Culturally Proficient Response to the Common Core: Ensuring Equity Through Professional Learning, 2015	Delores B. Lindsey Karen M. Kearney Delia Estrada Raymond D. Terrell Randall B. Lindsey	This book guides the reader to view and use the Common Core State Standards as a vehicle for ensuring all demographic groups of students are fully prepared for college and careers. • In what ways do I use this book to deepen my learning about equity? • In what ways do I use this book to deepen my learning about CCSS? • In what ways do I use this book with colleagues to deepen our work on equity and on the CCSS? • How can I and we use the Action Planning guide as an overlay for our current school planning?

Corwin Cultural Proficiency Books	Authors	Focus and Essential Questions
Culturally Proficient Inclusive Schools: All Means ALL! 2017	Delores B. Lindsey Jacqueline S. Thousand Cynthia L. Jew Lori R. Piowlski	This book provides responses and applications of the four Tools of Cultural Proficiency for educators who desire to create and support classrooms and schools that are inclusive and designed intentionally to educate all learners. General educators and Special Educators will benefit from using the 5 Essential Elements and the tenets of Inclusive Schooling to create and sustain educational environments so that when we say *all* students, we truly mean *all*! students will achieve at levels higher than ever before. Essential questions: • What might be some ways general and special educators can work collaboratively to create conditions for all students to be successful? • In what ways does this book address issues of equity and access for all students? • How do the four Tools of Cultural Proficiency inform the work of Inclusive Schooling? What's here for you? • In what ways does the Action Plan template offer opportunities for you and your colleagues? • For what are you waiting to help narrow and close equity gaps in your classroom and schools? • How do I foster challenging conversations about inclusive education with colleagues? • How do I extend my own learning about ways in which to facilitate inclusive learning environments?

(Continued)

(Continued)

Corwin Cultural Proficiency Books	Authors	Focus and Essential Questions
Fish Out of Water: Mentoring, Managing, and Self-Monitoring People Who Don't Fit In, 2016	Kikanza Nuri-Robins and Lewis Bundy	This book helps the reader manage the dynamics of difference by focusing on sustaining a healthy organizational culture using the Cultural Proficiency Continuum as a template. Strategies based on the Guiding Principles and the Essential Elements are provided for supporting both children and adults who are struggling to understand or use the cultural norms of a particular environment. A Study Guide is provided in the Resources so that the book can easily be used for professional development or a small group book study. • How do I determine the nature of diversity in this environment? • How might I understand who is thriving in this setting and who is not? • Are there any groups that are being targeted? • Are the rules of the environment oppressive to any individuals or groups in the environment? • Why are certain groups making the organizational rules for everyone? • How might I address systems to make the environment healthier? • What strategies are available to my colleagues and me as we seek to sustain a healthy, inclusive environment for all? • What strategies are available to an individual who is trying to succeed in a toxic environment? • How do I extend my own learning?

Corwin Cultural Proficiency Books	Authors	Focus and Essential Questions
Guiding Teams to Excellence with Equity: Culturally Proficient Facilitation, 2016	John Krownapple	This book provides mental models and information for educators to develop as facilitators of professional learning and organizational change for equity in education. It also supports experienced professional development professionals with tools for doing their work in a culturally competent and proficient manner. This book is for organizations working to build internal capacity and sustainability for Cultural Proficiency. Essential Questions: • Assuming we value excellence and equity in education, why do we need Cultural Proficiency and culturally proficient facilitators of the process? • How can we use Cultural Proficiency as content (framework) and process (journey) to achieve excellence with equity.? • What do facilitators do in order to work with teams in a culturally proficient manner?

Index

Achievement gap, 26–27, 36–37
Adaptive and technical change efforts, 14–16
Alpert, Dan, 2, 18
American Exceptionalism, 15
Angels in America (Kushner), 17
Anger-guilt continuum, 53–64
   carrying learning forward, 59–64
   entitlement reflections, 57–59
   overview, 53
   privilege and entitlement in, 54–57
Association of California School Administrators, 68

Barriers to cultural proficiency, 47–49
Beatty, B., 25
Bicultural groups, in marginalized populations, 50
Bigotry, motivation from expressions of, 16–17
Boese, Paul, 5
Brown v. Board of Education of Topeka (1954), 13, 24, 28
Bush, George W., 36

California's Public Accountability Act, 68
California State University, 11, 45
CampbellJones, Brenda, 25n
CampbellJones, F., 2
Change, resisting. *See* Anger-guilt continuum
Change efforts, adaptive and technical, 14–16
Change levers, disruption cycles as, 21–22
Chattel, 23
Civilian Conservation Corps, 8
Civil Rights Act of 1964, 14
Commitment and effort, 65–78
   essential elements of cultural competence in, 72–77
   guiding principles of cultural proficiency in, 68

inclusivity requiring, 67
   internal assets and intention in, 72
   overview, 65–66
   reflection and dialogue on, 68–72
Common Core Standards, 29
Communitycentric perceptions, 70
Conceptual Framework for Culturally Proficient Practices, 47, 50
Confidence, anger and guilt v., 55
Continuous improvement process, in cultural proficiency framework, 18
Cross, Terry, 3, 10–11, 14, 66, 68
Cultural assets, 47–49
Cultural blindness, 49
Cultural Competence model (Cross), 10–11, 14
Culturally Proficient Response to the Common Core, A (Lindsey, D. B; Kearney, Estrada, Terrell, and Lindsey, R. B.), 2, 81n
Culturally Proficient Schools (Lindsey, Roberts, and CampbellJones), 2
Cultural precompetence, 49
Cultural proficiency, introduction to, 1–4
Cultural proficiency framework, 47–50
Conceptual Framework for Culturally Proficient Practices, 47
   continuous improvement process in, 18
   equitable practices fostered by, 37–38
   equity focus from, 11–13
   leadership in, 43–46
   professional development in, 28
   rubric for cultural proficiency professional learning, 74–76
   school culture transformed by, 50–51
   tools in, 46–47

Declaration of Independence, 25
Deficit-focused efforts, 45

Desegregation of schools:
  Brown v. Board of Education of Topeka
      (1954), 13
  mandates versus educational needs in,
      20–21
  presidential election of 2016 and, 1–2
  Regional Assistance Center for
      Educational Equity, California State
      University, 11
  technical solutions to, 14, 45
Disruption cycles as change levers,
      21–22
Diversity, equitable educational
      opportunity and, 7–8
Domingues, Joseph, 1

Educational malpractice, 20
Eisenhower, Dwight D., 8
Elementary and Secondary Education
      Act of 1965, 24
Elementary and Secondary Education
      Act of 2002, 14, 24
Emergency School Aid Act, 14
Empathy, 53
Entitlement:
  oppression *v.*, 59–61
  privilege and, 54–57
  reflections on, 57–59
Equity. *See* Inequity and equity
Essential elements of cultural competence:
  commitment and effort guided by,
      72–77
  conceptual framework for culturally
      proficient practices, 48–49
  reflection on practices from, 63
  review of, 81t
  standards for educator behavior in,
      66–67
  tools of cultural proficiency including,
      12, 47
Estrada, D., 2, 81n

First Nations People, 23
Flores, Peter, III, 1
Founding documents, inequity and equity
      in, 24–26
Fullan, Michael, 20

Gladwell, M., 57
Guiding principles of cultural proficiency:
  conceptual framework for culturally
      proficient practices, 47–49
  Cross', 68
  overview, 12

reflecting on, 80
values in, 43
Guilt. *See* Anger-guilt continuum

Head Start, 24
Hilliard, Asa, 3, 9, 17, 41

Inclusivity, commitment and effort
      for, 67
Inequity and equity, 19–30
  achievement gaps, 26–27
  addressing, 22–24
  disruption cycles as change levers,
      21–22
  failing public schools, myth of, 27–29
  founding documents on, 24–26
  overview, 19–21
  school reform since 1980, 29–31
Interstate Highway System, 8

Jim Crow laws, 15, 26
Johnson, Lyndon B., 24

Kearney, K., 2, 81n
Kushner, Tony, 17

Lau v. Nichols (1974), 14, 24
Lawson, ??, 70
Leadership, 43–46
Leadership journal, 68
Lesbian, gay, bisexual, and transgender
      (LGBT) movement, 15
Lindsey, D. B., 1, 2, 44, 81n
Lindsey, R. B., 2, 81n

Manifesto, purpose of, 7–18
  bigotry expressions, motivation from,
      16–17
  book design, 18
  Cultural Proficiency Framework in,
      11–13
  overview, 7–8
  perspective on, 8–10
  technical and adaptive change efforts,
      14–16
  2016 election, concerns about, 10–11
Moral Imperative of Educational Leadership
      (Fullan), 20
Multiculturalism, 38

National Assessment of Educational
      Progress (NAEP), 3, 27
No Child Left Behind (NCLB) Act of 2002,
      3, 14, 36–37, 56, 68

Oppression, reactions to, 56, 59

Personal moral imperative, 60
Poverty, government avoidance of, 38
Privilege, entitlement and, 54–57

Regional Assistance Center for
    Educational Equity, 11
Regional Desegregation Center, California
    State University, 45
Resisting change. *See* Anger-guilt
    continuum
Rivers, I. D., 26, 28
Roberts, L. M., 2
Robins, Kikanza Nuri, 10, 14, 45, 68
Rubric for cultural proficiency professional
    learning, 74–76

San Marcos Elementary School (San
    Marcos, CA), 70
Schoolcentric perceptions, 70
Schools, 33–40
    achievement gap and, 36–37
    cultural transformation in, 50–51
    education language in, 33–36
    failing public schools, myth of, 27–29
    reform since 1980, 29–31
    second century of reform of, 37–38
    transformative change in, 36
    See also Desegregation of schools
Segregation, legalized, 15, 26
Self-determination, 60
Shields, C., 44

Six-Point Continuum of Cultural
    Proficiency, 12
Social justice education, 2
Span, C., 26, 28
"Sundown towns," 15

Tahoe Elementary School (Sacramento,
    CA), 70
Technical and adaptive change efforts,
    14–16
Terrell, Raymond D., 1, 10, 14, 45,
    68, 81n
Tools of cultural proficiency, 11–12
Transactional leadership, 44
Transformational leadership, 44
Transformative leadership, 44
2016 election:
    concerns about, 10–11
    discord unleashed by, 7, 21–22
    hostility toward marginalized groups
        and, 15, 35

University of Illinois, 19
Urban impact money, 45
U.S. Office for Civil Rights, 13
U.S. Supreme Court:
    Brown v. Board of Education of Topeka
        (1954), 13, 24, 28
    Lau v. Nichols (1974), 14, 24

War on Poverty, 24
Weick, K., 44
Women's suffrage, 23

A SAGE Publishing Company

Helping educators make the greatest impact

CORWIN HAS ONE MISSION: to enhance education through intentional professional learning.

We build long-term relationships with our authors, educators, clients, and associations who partner with us to develop and continuously improve the best evidence-based practices that establish and support lifelong learning.

Solutions you want. Experts you trust. Results you need.